Vegetables

Christian
Teubner

Vegetables

BARRON'S

Woodbury, New York • London • Toronto • Sydney

First English-language edition published 1986 by
Barron's Educational Series, Inc.

© 1985 by Grafe und Unzer GmbH, Munich, West Germany

The title of the German edition is *Gemüse*.

All inquiries should be addressed to:
Barron's Educational Series, Inc.
113 Crossways Park Drive
Woodbury, New York 11797

Library of Congress Catalog Card No. 86-10772

International Standard Book No. 0-8120-5735-X

Library of Congress Cataloging-in-Publication Data

Teubner, Christian.
    Vegetables.

    (Magic cooking series)
    Translation of: Gemüse.
    Includes index.
    1. Cookery (Vegetables) I. Title. II. Series.
TX801.T4813 1986   641.6′5   86-10772
ISBN 0-8120-5735-X

Color photographs by Christian Teubner

Translation and Americanization by Patricia Connell

PRINTED IN HONG KONG

6 7 8 9   9 8 7 6 5 4 3 2 1

CONTENTS

PREFACE

The subject of this illustrated book is one of the most interesting and healthful areas in all cookery. Accomplished cooks everywhere agree that fresh vegetables allow fabulous scope for creativity in the kitchen —and fresh is the only kind you will see in these recipes. These days the selection of vegetables is so vast that choosing the right one can become a problem in itself. With my tips and recipe ideas I hope to be of help, and to demonstrate that vegetables are not only good accompaniments but can also make splendid main dishes.

Variety is the spice of good cooking (hardly a new discovery!) and vegetables have much to offer in this regard. Kitchen gardening was already in full bloom as far back as ancient Egypt, where vegetables —among them cucumbers, peas, green beans, and onions —were important staple foods. The classical Roman kitchen also used vegetables of many kinds. Apicius devotes a whole chapter of his renowned cookbook to them, even providing a recipe for ferns; and asparagus, already prized in antiquity, was cultivated around Ravenna.

Because food is so dependent on climate, Italian chefs have always given vegetables a starring role. Italian cookery has also had a lasting influence on French cuisine. By the Renaissance the French were already experienced in vegetable cultivation, and New World varieties such as tomatoes, potatoes, peppers, and corn rapidly became naturalized to the Mediterranean climate. Nor must we forget Oriental cooking, with its masterful treatment of fresh vegetables.

In northern European and American cooking, on the other hand, vegetables were for hundreds of years sorely neglected. Relegated to a minor role in the meal, vegetables were only considered a main course when cooked with a hunk of meat; otherwise they constituted "poor people's food," a role that was reinforced by the limited selection available.

Happily, vegetables have now taken their rightful place in the forefront of modern cooking. The purpose of this book is to show how versatile, varied, and delicious fresh vegetables can be. There are recipes for all manner of readily available vegetables as well as some less familiar kinds; there are unusual preparations and old favorites. The recipes are preceded by general information about the category at large—root and bulb vegetables, leaf vegetables, the cabbage and onion families, and so on.

I hope you are already a fan of fresh vegetables and that with these new recipes your enthusiasm will grow. *Bon appétit!*

BASICS OF VEGETABLE COOKERY

Today vegetables are prized not only as tasty side dishes but as excellent entrées. You will find both kinds of recipes in this book. Should you wish to convert a side dish to an entrée, merely plan on serving fewer persons or double the recipe.

Fresh is Best

In recent years the selection of vegetables at supermarkets and produce stands has grown far larger than ever before—a welcome development, because the flavor of fresh vegetables is incomparably better than that of frozen or canned. Many fresh vegetables also enjoy a much longer season than they used to, since they are now imported from Mexico, Israel, and other areas with different or longer growing seasons than our own. From a nutritional point of view it has become more and more clear what an important role unprocessed vegetables play in the diet, for they are rich in essential vitamins, minerals, trace elements, and fiber.

Be sure that the vegetables you buy at the greengrocer's are truly fresh, not limp remnants of a delivery from days before.

And get them home as soon as possible after purchase—particularly leaf vegetables, which are especially prone to wilting. Only cabbage and root vegetables can be kept a few days without deteriorating in flavor and texture.

Knowing and Using Seasonal Vegetables

The huge selection of vegetables in any well-stocked market sometimes makes us forget that most domestically grown tomatoes, for example, hang ripe on the vine only in late summer and early fall. Imported or hothouse-grown tomatoes are available year round, but are more expensive and may be quite tasteless. It is nearly impossible for the average consumer to determine which tomatoes are actually sun-ripened and which are forced in a greenhouse. It is not enough that they be plump and red; they must also have flavor.

The surest way of getting fresh, locally grown produce is to buy when prices are at their lowest. When a given vegetable is most abundant and cheapest in the market you have the best guarantee that it is in season and consequently at its best possible quality. I have noted in the introduction to each vegetable type when it is in its high season.

Fresh Vegetables: Worth the Effort

It takes a little more trouble to prepare fresh vegetables, since you will have to spend a few minutes washing, trimming, peeling, and slicing—but it is effort that is amply repaid. While frozen and canned vegetables save time, they are no substitute for those that are fresh and properly prepared.

To best preserve flavor and nutrients, do not soak vegetables—just wash them briefly—and slice or chop them as soon as possible before cooking. Above all, cook them no longer than absolutely necessary. Take careful note of the cooking times in the recipes and test the vegetables several times as they cook, because particularly young or tender vegetables will be ready sooner. Most kinds of vegetables taste best when cooked just until crisp-tender, retaining a pleasantly firm "bite" to the tooth.

PEAS AND BEANS

Peas

Peas are a standard—and highly nutritious—vegetable in American menus. Both the pea itself (that is, the seed) and its pod are a storehouse of the proteins, minerals, and carbohydrates needed by the plant for its development.

Unfortunately, sweet fresh peas have been almost completely driven out of the markets by their frozen counterparts. But they are starting to make a comeback, particularly at farmers' markets, where they are most plentiful from early June until the middle of August.

Choicest of all are snow peas and sugar snap peas, with completely edible pods and sweet seed kernels. Snow peas have a delightfully fresh, delicate flavor and need only the briefest of cooking times.

Fresh Pea Skillet

Serve with boiled potatoes for a complete meal. Peas prepared in this manner are also very good as an accompaniment to meat dishes.

4 servings
1¼ pounds (600 g) shelled fresh peas
1 onion
1 small parsley root
3 tablespoons (40 g) butter
1 cup (240 mL) meat stock
¼ teaspoon salt
Freshly ground pepper
6 ounces (180 g) bacon
1 generous tablespoon chopped fresh parsley
2 teaspoons chopped lovage or celery leaves
1 egg

Depending on the type of peas, you will need to buy at least 2 ½ pounds (1200 g) unshelled peas to get 1¼ pounds (600 g) shelled. Peel and finely chop onion. Carefully clean parsley root and chop finely. Melt butter in large skillet, add onion and parsley root, and sauté over medium heat until tender. Add peas and cook 2 to 3 minutes. Pour in stock. Season peas with salt and pepper and cook uncovered over medium heat until liquid is nearly evaporated, 15 to 20 minutes.

Meanwhile, slice bacon into fine strips and brown in another skillet, stirring constantly. Stir into peas with chopped herbs. Break egg over peas and immediately remove from heat. Stir through several times; the retained heat will be sufficient to cook the egg.

Peas with Cheese Sauce

Not illustrated

4 servings
1¼ pounds (600 g) shelled fresh peas
l cup (240 mL) chicken stock
For the sauce
3 strips (50 g) bacon
½ cup (125 mL) heavy cream
2 egg yolks
2 tablespoons chopped fresh parsley
½ teaspoon salt
¾ cup (80 g) grated Emmenthal cheese
½ cup (125 mL) chicken stock

Cook shelled peas in 1 cup (240 mL) chicken stock over medium heat for about 15 minutes.

Meanwhile, finely dice bacon and render in heavy saucepan. Stir in cream and remove from heat. Whisk in yolks, parsley and salt. Add cheese and ½ cup (125 mL) chicken stock and cook over very low heat until sauce is thickened and smooth; *do not boil* or sauce will curdle. Stir in hot peas and serve immediately.

French-style Peas

Photo, top

These tender, moist peas go well with briefly cooked meats.

4 servings
6 small shallots
3 tablespoons (40 g) butter
1 teaspoon salt
1/2 teaspoon sugar
4 parsley stalks
1/4 cup (60 mL) water
1 small head leaf lettuce
12 ounces (400 g) shelled fresh peas

Peel shallots. Melt butter in large saucepan, add whole shallots, and sauté over moderate heat until translucent. Sprinkle with salt and sugar, add parsley, and pour water over. Cover and cook gently 10 minutes. Remove outer leaves from lettuce and reserve for another use. Wash and drain lettuce heart; cut into quarters. Tie quarters together with cotton thread. Add to shallots and cover with peas. Cover saucepan and cook 10 minutes. Remove thread from lettuce and discard parsley stems. Shake pan to distribute vegetables evenly; taste and adjust seasoning.

Snow Peas

Be sure the snow peas you buy are absolutely fresh; only then will they stay crisp and flavorful after cooking. Snow peas are most abundant in May and June, but in many areas are available year round—at a substantial price.

Snow Peas with Truffles

Of course, the delicious (and fabulously expensive) truffle can be omitted and the snow peas will still be delicious. They make an excellent accompaniment to nearly any meat or fish dish.

Photo, bottom

4 servings
1 1/4 pounds (600 g) snow peas
Salt
6 shallots
1 clove garlic
1/4 cup (60 g) butter
1 tablespoon chopped fresh parsley
1 canned truffle

Briefly wash snow peas. Snap off stem ends, pulling off as much as possible of the string that runs the length of the snow pea. Repeat at pointed end of each pod, removing remainder of string. Bring large amount of salted water to boil, add snow peas, and boil briskly for 3 minutes. Remove and drain well. Peel and mince shallots; peel garlic and force through garlic press. Melt butter in large saucepan, add shallots and garlic, and sauté until tender but not colored. Add snow peas, and cook, stirring, 4 to 5 minutes. Stir in parsley. Cut truffle into paper-thin slices and add as the final touch.

Green Beans

There are numerous kinds of green beans, the most important of which are the bush or dwarf types and the climbing varieties. Either growth habit can produce green snap beans or the flat-podded Italian beans. Among the snap beans are the yellow ones known as wax beans. Snap beans can be cut, or as the name implies, broken into several pieces before cooking. In modern hybrids the tough string is virtually nonexistent. Broad-podded beans, while particularly flavorful, do not have a string that must be pulled away before slicing; they are then cut with a knife rather than being "snapped" into pieces.

Fresh green beans are most widely available from May to October, but thanks to imports they can be purchased nearly year round.

Green Beans with Ground Meat

Photo, top

4 servings
1 generous pound (500 g) young green beans
Salt
1 large red bell pepper
2 large tomatoes
1 medium onion
1 clove garlic
3 tablespoons vegetable oil
12 ounces (350 g) mixed ground meat
1 tablespoon sweet paprika
1 cup (240 mL) meat stock (or more if needed)
1 tablespoon chopped fresh parsley

Trim ends from beans and remove strings if necessary. Drop beans into large quantity of boiling salted water and boil 10 minutes; drain. Halve and seed bell pepper and cut into strips. Blanch tomatoes briefly in boiling water; peel, halve, seed, and dice. Peel and chop onion. Peel garlic and crush in garlic press. Heat oil in large saucepan. Add onion and garlic and sauté until tender. Add meat and paprika with 1 teaspoon salt and stir over high heat 5 minutes. Add tomatoes and stock, reduce heat, and simmer 10 minutes. Stir in beans and pepper strips and simmer 15 minutes longer, adding more stock if necessary. Sprinkle with parsley and serve.

Savory Green Beans

Photo, bottom

4 servings
1 generous pound (500 g) young green beans
Salt
2 small onions
1/4 cup (60 mL) vegetable oil
1 tablespoon chopped fresh parsley
2 teaspoons chopped fresh savory
1/2 teaspoon chopped fresh sage

Trim ends from beans and remove strings if necessary. Bring large quantity of salted water to boil in saucepan. Add beans and cook until crisp-tender, 15 to 20 minutes. Drain and plunge into ice water to stop cooking process and retain bright green color. Meanwhile, peel and slice onions. Heat oil in large skillet. Add onions and sauté until light golden, stirring frequently. Add beans and cook 5 to 10 minutes longer. Sprinkle with chopped herbs, cover, and cook for a few minutes over low heat to blend flavors.

Mixed Bean Chili

Beans originated in Central and South America, and these areas still boast an exceptional variety of recipes for both the fresh and dried types. *Chili con Carne* is a meat-based bean stew that exists in countless variations, this time featuring both dried and fresh beans.

4 servings
1 generous pound (500 g) dried kidney beans
1 generous pound (500 g) tomatoes
3 small carrots
1 large onion
2 cloves garlic
7 tablespoons vegetable oil
2 to 4 fresh red chili peppers
1 generous pound (500 g) beef brisket or stew meat
1 cup (240 mL) meat stock
1 generous pound (500 g) fresh Italian green beans
1 teaspoon salt
2 teaspoons sweet paprika
1/2 teaspoon chopped fresh thyme
1 tablespoon chopped fresh parsley

Cover beans generously with cold water and soak overnight.

Blanch tomatoes briefly in boiling water, then peel, stem, seed, and dice. Peel and chop onion. Peel garlic and crush in garlic press. Clean and dice carrots.

Heat 4 tablespoons oil in large skillet, add onion and garlic, and sauté until tender. Halve chili peppers and discard stem and seeds. Finely dice peppers. (Wash hands immediately after chopping peppers, as their pungent oils can irritate the skin.) Add chilies, carrot, and tomato to onion in skillet and simmer 10 minutes; remove from heat and keep warm. Cut meat into small cubes. Heat remaining 3 tablespoons oil in another skillet. Add meat and sauté over high heat until browned on all sides, about 5 minutes. Add tomato mixture and drained kidney beans to meat with stock. Wash and trim green beans, removing strings if necessary. Cut beans into small pieces.

Add to skillet and season with salt, paprika, thyme, and parsley. Simmer over low heat until meat is tender and kidney beans are cooked through, about 1 1/2 hours.

Green Beans and Squash

Not illustrated

4 servings
1 1/4 pounds (600 g) fresh Italian green beans
Salt
2 1/4-pound (1-kg) winter squash, such as butternut or acorn
1 generous pound (500 g) tomatoes
1 medium onion
1 clove garlic
1/2 cup (125 mL) olive oil
1/2 cup (125 mL) white wine
1 tablespoon chopped fresh basil
Freshly ground pepper

Wash beans, trim ends, and remove strings if necessary. Cut beans into pieces. Bring large quantity of salted water to boil, add beans, and cook 20 minutes. Peel squash deeply; discard seeds and strings. Cut squash into 1/2-inch (1 1/2-cm) cubes. Blanch tomatoes briefly in boiling water; peel, seed, and dice into similar-size cubes. Peel and chop onion; peel and crush garlic. Heat oil in large saucepan. Add onion and garlic and sauté until tender. Add beans, squash, and tomato, and pour in wine. Season with 1 teaspoon salt, the basil, and pepper. Cover and simmer over very low heat until vegetables are tender, about 40 minutes.

DELECTABLE ASPARAGUS

Among the oldest of cultivated vegetables, asparagus originated in the Near East and was already prized by the ancient Greeks and Romans. Today it grows wild all over the Mediterranean.

Asparagus has become popular around the world, and it is grown wherever the climate and soil are suitable for its cultivation. The vegetable's appeal for gourmets has fortunately not been quelled by the mushy canned version available in every market. Thanks to modern cultivation techniques, fresh asparagus is of outstanding quality when purchased in season (from the beginning of May through the end of June). Connoisseurs can never agree which is best—the pristine, all-white type popular in Germany, white with violet tips grown in France; or the green asparagus popular in Italy and America. But this is a question of personal preference; any fresh asparagus, properly cooked, is a treat.

Asparagus recipes could fill a good-sized cookbook, so this book includes only the basics of preparing this unique vegetable. It goes well with all manner of highly flavored ingredients such as prosciutto, country ham, or smoked salmon. Hard-cooked eggs, an herbed vinaigrette, or hollandaise sauce are also wonderful accompaniments. But purists prefer asparagus with nothing more than a pat of butter, and with good reason; nothing makes a better complement to its fine flavor.

Buttered Asparagus

4 servings
4¹/2 pounds (2 kg) fresh asparagus
Salt
¹/2 teaspoon sugar
Butter

Not everyone agrees as to whether asparagus should be washed. In fact, the best treatment is to rinse the tips under cold running water and then to peel any thick stalks; pencil-thin green asparagus need not be peeled. The fresher the asparagus, the thinner the layer of skin that must be peeled away. Starting from about ³/4 inch (2 cm) beneath the tip, use a vegetable peeler to remove the skin, peeling toward the base of the stalk. Break off about ³/4 inch (2 cm) from the base of the stalk, as it is usually woody. (An excellent broth can be prepared from the washed peelings and trimmings.) Using cotton thread, tie asparagus into small bunches. Place in enough lightly salted boiling water to cover the asparagus completely. Add sugar. Simmer the asparagus for 15 to 20 minutes, depending on thickness; test a stalk frequently during cooking, removing the pan from the heat when the stalks are crisp-tender (the asparagus should not be hard, but never let it overcook and become mushy). Drain well on paper towels, then untie the bundles and serve with butter or a sauce.

A special treat for asparagus lovers is a serving of white and green stalks combined. Drizzle with melted butter or let a pat of butter melt over the asparagus, as you prefer.

LEAFY VEGETABLES

Spinach

Happily, fresh spinach is now available year round. There are, however, different varieties: Tender, light green spinach has especially fine flavor, while dark spinach often has coarser, more crinkled leaves and a stronger taste. Depending on the exact type of spinach and on where it is purchased, it may come in the form of individual leaves or as whole clusters that must be picked over and stemmed; naturally there is more waste in the latter type.

Spinach is a universal and infinitely adaptable vegetable. It can be made into outstanding soups, it lends itself to use in delicious stuffings, and of course it is most popular of all as a side dish. It is particularly beloved in Italian cooking, where it even appears as a main course.

Italian-style Spinach

Excellent as a side dish, particularly when paired with garlic bread or potato gnocchi.

4 servings
$^1/_4$ cup (40 g) raisins
$^1/_4$ cup (60 mL) sweet white wine
2$^1/_4$ pounds (1 kg) spinach
1 tablespoon vegetable oil
2 green onions
$^1/_4$ clove garlic
3 tablespoons (50 g) butter
3 anchovy fillets
6 tablespoons (50 g) pine nuts
1 tablespoon chopped fresh parsley
Salt and freshly ground pepper
Freshly grated nutmeg

Soften raisins in slightly warmed white wine. Pick over spinach, discarding thick stems. Wash in several changes of water and drain well in strainer or colander. Heat oil in large saucepan, add spinach, and stir until wilted, about 2 minutes. Remove from heat and drain in sieve. Trim and mince green onions. Crush garlic (there really should be only $^1/_4$ clove of garlic at most; the dish should betray only a hint of it.)

Melt butter in saucepan, add green onion and garlic, and sauté briefly. Add crushed anchovies, pine nuts, and chopped parsley. Stir in raisins with wine and cook gently 3 to 4 minutes. Add drained spinach. Season with salt, pepper, and nutmeg and cook over very low heat 8 to 12 minutes.

Variation
Spinach Gratin

Prepare spinach according to previous recipe. When all ingredients are combined, spread in gratin dish. Place in preheated 425°F (220°C) oven for 5 minutes. Combine $^3/_4$ cup (100 g) freshly grated Parmesan cheese and 1 cup (240 mL) heavy cream and pour over spinach. Sprinkle with an additional $^3/_4$ cup (100 g) grated Parmesan and dot with $^1/_3$ cup (80 g) butter. Bake until top is crusty and golden brown, about 10 minutes longer. Serve immediately.

Swiss Chard Soup

For this recipe only the leaves of the chard are used. Peel the stalks and prepare them as a side dish with another meal.

4 servings
2¼ pounds (1 kg) Swiss chard
1 small onion
3 tablespoons (40 g) butter
1 teaspoon salt
Freshly ground pepper
Chopped fresh basil
3 cups (700 mL) meat stock
2 ripe tomatoes
7 tablespoons (100 g) crème fraîche

Cut chard leaves into strips. Peel and mince onion. Melt butter in large saucepan, add onion, and sauté until translucent. Add chard leaves and cook until wilted, 3 to 4 minutes. Season with salt, pepper, and basil. Pour in meat stock and heat slowly. Blanch tomatoes briefly in boiling water; peel, seed, and dice. Add to saucepan and simmer 10 minutes. Adjust seasoning, whisk in crème fraîche, and serve.

Watercress Soup

Photo, center

4 servings
2 large leeks, white part only
1 small onion
½ clove garlic
3 tablespoons (40 g) butter
1 large potato
1 quart (1 L) chicken stock
3 bunches watercress
½ teaspoon salt
Freshly ground pepper
Grated fresh ginger
½ cup (125 mL) dry white wine

Wash leek thoroughly, peel onion, and mince both. Force garlic through garlic press. Melt butter; add leek, onion, and garlic and sauté until tender. Peel and dice potato and add to leek mixture. Pour in chicken stock and simmer 15 minutes. Wash and drain watercress; discard thick stems and add leaves to soup. Season with salt, pepper, and ginger and simmer until potato disintegrates. Puree soup in batches in processor or blender. Return to saucepan, add wine, and heat through briefly to blend flavors. Serve hot.

Sorrel Soup

Photo, top

4 servings
1 small to medium onion
1 small potato
½ cup (60 g) trimmed celery
3 tablespoons (40 g) butter
¼ cup (60 mL) white wine
8 ounces (250 g) sorrel
1 tablespoon fresh lemon juice
1 teaspoon salt
Freshly ground pepper
Freshly grated nutmeg
3 cups (700 mL) meat stock
1 egg yolk
½ cup (125 mL) heavy cream
Toasted croutons

Peel and mince onion and potato; mince celery. Melt butter, add vegetables and wine, and cook over low heat 15 minutes. Discard thick stems from sorrel and wash leaves well. Add leaves (with water clinging to them) to onion mixture and cook until completely wilted. Stir in lemon juice, salt, pepper, and nutmeg. Pour in stock and simmer 10 to 15 minutes. Whisk egg yolk with cream and whisk into soup to thicken slightly. Heat through, but do not boil or yolk will curdle. Ladle soup into bowls, sprinkle with croutons, and serve.

Belgian Endive

Belgian endive is a "noble" relative of the coarser chicory whose root was once used as a coffee substitute. A Belgian gardener discovered that these roots, when cultivated in darkness, would send up fresh leaves during the winter months. Thanks to ever more sophisticated growing techniques, endive has developed into a refined vegetable that is usually made into a salad but is also superb when served hot.

Belgian endive is most widely available in the fall and winter months. Buy only crisp, firm heads, avoiding any whose leaves are tipped with brown. They will keep in the crisper drawer of your refrigerator for at least one week; if necessary, remove any leaves that have discolored during storage. If you do not like the typically bitter taste of endive, remove the core with a cone-shaped cut—but the fact is that the newer cultivars have very little bitterness. Use enameled or stainless-steel saucepans, for endive will darken unappetizingly in aluminum or iron cookware.

Stuffed Endive

Serve with fresh tomato sauce (see recipe, page 58) and boiled new potatoes.

4 servings
8 medium heads of Belgian endive (about $1^1/_4$ to $1^1/_2$ pounds / 600 to 700 g)
Juice of 1 lemon
$^1/_2$ teaspoon salt
8 strips (200 g) thinly sliced bacon
3 tablespoons (50 g) butter
$^1/_2$ cup (125 mL) white wine
$^1/_2$ cup (125 mL) meat stock
For the stuffing
1 small onion
2 tablespoons (30 g) butter
8 ounces (250 g) lean ground pork
1 egg
Salt and freshly ground pepper
Pinch of freshly grated nutmeg
1 teaspoon sweet paprika
1 tablespoon chopped fresh parsley
1 tablespoon breadcrumbs

Cut away lower part of endive core with cone-shaped cut; halve heads lengthwise. Arrange on work surface with cut sides up; remove small interior leaves and set aside. Rub cut sides with lemon juice and sprinkle with salt.

Peel and mince onion for stuffing. Melt butter in large saucepan, add onion, and sauté until tender. Finely chop reserved small endive leaves, add to onion, and cook until wilted, about 2 minutes. Combine ground pork with egg, salt, pepper, nutmeg, paprika, parsley, and breadcrumbs in mixing bowl. Add onion mixture and blend well. Divide mixture among 8 endive halves, spreading top level. Top with remaining 8 halves. Wrap each with a bacon slice. Melt butter in flameproof oven dish or gratin pan. Place stuffed endive in dish with ends of bacon strips underneath to keep stuffing from falling out (endive can also be secured with toothpicks if necessary). Bake in preheated 400°F (200°C) oven for 20 to 25 minutes, pouring mixed wine and stock over endive after the first 5 minutes; add more stock during baking if liquid evaporates.

Grape Leaves

Grape leaves have been beloved in Mediterranean kitchens since ancient times. They are not usually available fresh in this country, but they can be purchased at Middle Eastern markets—look for them canned or bottled, packed in brine or oil.

Rice-stuffed Grape Leaves

Photo, bottom

4 servings
1 small onion
3 tablespoons olive oil
1 scant cup (150 g) rice
1 cup (240 mL) meat or chicken stock
6 tablespoons (50 g) chopped almonds
6 tablespoons (50 g) pine nuts
2 tablespoons chopped fresh parsley
1 teaspoon chopped fresh mint leaves
1/2 teaspoon salt
1 teaspoon sugar
Freshly ground pepper
7 ounces (200 g) grape leaves
1/2 cup (125 mL) white wine
2 tablespoons fresh lemon juice

Peel and chop onion. Heat olive oil in large saucepan, add onion, and sauté until translucent. Add rice and stir over medium heat for several minutes. Stir in stock, almonds, pine nuts, herbs, salt, sugar, and pepper; cook until rice has absorbed all liquid.

Spread out grape leaves individually on work surface. Mound 1 rounded tablespoon rice mixture on each leaf. Starting from stem end, roll up each grape leaf halfway, then tuck in sides of leaf and finish rolling to completely enclose stuffing. Oil baking dish large enough to hold stuffed leaves. Arrange leaves in dish and pour mixed wine and lemon juice over. Cover with lid or foil and bake in preheated 400°F (200°C) oven for about 25 minutes. Serve hot.

Lamb-stuffed Grape Leaves

Filling in photo, top

4 servings
1 small onion
1 clove garlic
12 ounces (400 g) lean trimmed lamb shoulder or leg
2 tablespoons olive oil
1/2 teaspoon salt
1 teaspoon sweet paprika
Freshly ground pepper
1 tablespoon chopped fresh parsley
1 teaspoon chopped fresh sage
1/2 teaspoon chopped fresh thyme
A few rosemary leaves
1 large tomato
3/4 cup cooked rice
7 ounces (200 g) grape leaves
1/2 cup (125 mL) meat stock

Peel and finely chop onion and garlic. Finely dice lamb. Heat oil in skillet, add onion and garlic, and sauté until tender. Add lamb and stir until browned on all sides, about 5 minutes. Season with salt, paprika, pepper, and herbs. Blanch tomato briefly in boiling water; peel, seed, dice, and add to lamb. Cook over medium heat for 10 minutes, stirring frequently. Stir in rice. Stuff grape leaves as in preceding recipe, arrange in oiled baking dish, and pour meat stock over. Cover and bake in preheated 400°F (200°C) oven for 25 to 30 minutes.

FENNEL, ARTICHOKES, CELERY

Fennel

The ancient Egyptians and Greeks used wild fennel as a votive offering, and by Roman times it was prized as a food for mortals, too. Even today, wild fennel still appears in Sicilian *Pasta con le Sarde,* pasta with fennel greens and sardines.

Cultivated fennel also has a long history in Mediterranean cooking, but is only now becoming familiar to many American cooks. Its crisp, fresh texture and refreshing anise flavor make it a wonderful accompaniment to many meat and poultry entrées.

Though available throughout much of the year, fennel is chiefly a winter vegetable and is usually at its best during the colder months.

Fennel à la Grecque

Photo, bottom

4 servings
1¼ pounds (600 g) fennel bulbs
1 clove garlic
1 large onion
3 tablespoons olive oil
2 ripe tomatoes
½ cup (125 mL) white wine
10 ounces (300 g) veal rump or round
½ teaspoon salt
Freshly ground pepper
1 teaspoon sweet paprika
1 cup (240 mL) meat stock
2 tablespoons crème fraîche
1 tablespoon chopped fennel greens

Trim and wash fennel, removing any tough stalks or outer layers. Cut bulbs into coarse chunks. Peel garlic and onion; crush garlic and mince onion. Heat olive oil in large saucepan, add garlic and onion, and sauté until tender. Blanch tomatoes briefly in boiling water; skin, halve, seed, and chop coarsely. Add tomato and wine to onion mixture and cook over high heat 5 minutes. Cut veal into small cubes and add to saucepan; cook 5 minutes. Add fennel, salt, pepper, paprika, and stock; cover and simmer gently over low heat 30 to 40 minutes. Just before serving, stir in crème fraîche and sprinkle with chopped fennel greens.

Fennel with Cream and Parmesan

Photo, top

4 servings
1½ pounds (750 g) fennel bulbs
Salt
¼ cup (60 g) butter
½ cup (125 mL) heavy cream
Freshly ground pepper
¾ cup (100 g) freshly grated Parmesan cheese

Trim and wash fennel, removing any tough outer layers. Cut off stalks near bulb. Halve bulbs (or quarter if very large). Drop fennel into large saucepan of lightly salted boiling water and cook 10 minutes, then drain well. Melt butter in flameproof gratin dish. Add fennel and sauté briefly on top of stove. Pour cream over, season with salt and pepper, and sprinkle with cheese. Bake in preheated 375°F (190°C) until cheese is golden, about 15 to 20 minutes. Serve immediately.

Sausage-stuffed Fennel

Photo, bottom

Excellent with the tomato sauce on page 58. Accompany with rice or boiled potatoes.

4 servings
1 3/4 pounds (800 g) fennel bulbs
Salt
3 tablespoons (50 g) butter
1/2 cup (50 g) freshly grated Parmesan cheese
2 tablespoons breadcrumbs
1/4 cup (60 mL) meat stock
For the stuffing
7 ounces (200 g) uncooked bratwurst
3 ounces (100 g) boiled ham
1 clove garlic
2 tablespoons minced onion
1 tablespoon chopped fresh parsley
2/3 cup (150 g) crème fraîche

Trim and wash fennel; trim stalks short and remove any tough outer layers. Halve fennel bulbs. Bring large saucepan of salted water to boil, add fennel and boil 8 minutes. Remove and drain well. Melt butter in flameproof gratin dish.

For the filling, press bratwurst out of its casing. Finely chop ham. Peel and crush garlic. Combine sausage, ham, garlic, chopped onion, and parsley, then stir in crème fraîche. Divide stuffing among cut sides of fennel bulbs. Mix Parmesan and breadcrumbs and scatter over stuffing. Arrange fennel in buttered gratin dish, stuffed side up. Pour in stock. Bake in preheated 400°F (210°C) oven for 15 to 20 minutes.

Deep-fried Fennel

Photo, top

Serve with tomato sauce.

4 servings
1 1/4 pounds (600 g) fennel bulbs
Salt
1 cup (125 g) all-purpose flour
2 eggs, separated
1/4 teaspoon salt
Pinch of freshly grated nutmeg
1/2 cup (125 mL) beer
Vegetable oil for deep-frying

Trim and wash fennel bulbs, removing any tough outer layers. Cut away stalks. Cut bulb into 3/8-inch (1-cm) slices; separate slices into individual segments. Drop fennel pieces into large saucepan of boiling salted water and boil for 3 to 4 minutes. Remove and drain well.

For the batter, combine flour, egg yolks, salt, nutmeg, and beer in mixing bowl and blend until smooth. Beat egg whites to soft peaks and fold into batter with whisk.

Heat oil in large saucepan or deep-fryer to 350°F (180°C). Pierce fennel pieces with fork and dip into batter to coat completely; immediately drop into hot oil. Fry until golden brown on both sides, turning once. Remove with slotted spoon and drain well on paper towels. Serve hot.

Artichokes

This noble cousin of the thistle is becoming more and more popular in American kitchens. Artichokes are most abundant in spring and fall; depending on age and variety, they can weigh anywhere from about 5 ounces to over a pound (150 to 500 g). Choose those with tight, firm leaves and without brown spots.

Basic Boiled Artichokes

Typically served with vinaigrette or a mayonnaise sauce, boiled artichokes are a perfect first course. If you serve two or three good-size artichokes per person and accompany them with crusty French or Italian bread, they make a delicious light entrée.

Wash artichokes and trim stem end, immediately rubbing with lemon juice to prevent discoloration. Remove outermost layer of leaves and, if desired, trim away thorny tip of each remaining leaf with kitchen shears. Drop artichokes into large pot of boiling salted water and cook about 30 to 40 minutes, depending on size; they are done when a leaf comes away easily. During cooking the artichokes open somewhat, making it easier to scoop out the inedible hairy choke. (Remove the choke before serving or have each diner do it at the table, as you prefer.)

To eat artichokes, pull off each leaf individually, dip into sauce, and pull between the teeth to scrape off the tender flesh, holding the leaf by the tip. Remove choke, if still present, and then eat the meaty artichoke bottom with a knife and fork.

Among the countless artichoke preparations known to cooks the world over, the following—artichokes Roman style—is a classic.

Carciofi alla Romana

6 servings
6 large artichokes
Juice of 1 lemon
2 cloves garlic
1 bunch parsley
3 tablespoons olive oil
2 tablespoons chopped shallot
1 tablespoon chopped fresh mint
1 cup (50 g) breadcrumbs
1/4 teaspoon salt
Freshly ground pepper
1/2 cup (125 mL) olive oil
Chicken stock or water

Remove tough outer leaves from artichokes; cut away thorny tips from remaining leaves with kitchen shears. Trim stalk, leaving about 1 1/4 to 1 1/2 inches (3 to 4 cm); cut off top of artichoke (use stainless steel knife to keep cut surfaces from darkening). Immediately drop artichokes into large bowl of water mixed with the lemon juice to prevent discoloration.

Peel and crush garlic; chop parsley. Heat 3 tablespoons olive oil in skillet. Add shallot and garlic and sauté briefly. Stir in parsley, mint, breadcrumbs, salt, and pepper; remove from heat.

Remove artichokes from water, drain, and pat dry. Open up leaves to expose hairy choke; remove choke with spoon. Divide stuffing among artichoke centers and gently press closed. Heat 1/2 cup (125 mL) olive oil in heavy large ovenproof skillet, preferably cast iron; arrange artichokes side by side in skillet with stalks up. Pour enough chicken stock or water into skillet to come 1/3 up sides of artichokes. Bake in preheated 400°F (200°C) oven for 30 to 40 minutes, covering stalks with aluminum foil if they become too dark. Serve warm or cold as a first course.

Celery

Celery adds a note of crisp greenness to the produce bins winter and summer alike; while October through April could be considered its "high" season, one or another type of celery is widely available year round. This refreshing vegetable is often prepared as a salad, and the English like to serve the crisp raw stalks with afternoon tea. But it may also be cooked and served hot. Braising is a typical preparation, and so is stuffing; celery may, for example, be substituted for squash in the recipe for Stuffed Zucchini on page 46.

Braised Celery

Photo, bottom

4 servings
2¹/₄ pounds (1 kg) celery
2 shallots
3 tablespoons (50 g) butter
1 tablespoon fresh lemon juice
¹/₂ teaspoon salt
Freshly ground pepper
1 cup (240 mL) chicken stock
3 to 4 tablespoons crème fraîche (optional)
1 tablespoon chopped fresh parsley

Trim and wash celery, cutting away bottom end of stalk and the leaves, which are bitter. Cut stalks into pieces about 5 inches (12 cm) long; if very thick, halve or quarter the stalks lengthwise. Peel and mince shallot. Melt butter in large saucepan, add shallot, and sauté briefly. Add celery, salt, pepper, and chicken stock. Cover and braise over medium-low heat, stirring frequently, about 20 minutes. If desired, stir in crème fraîche to enrich braising liquid. Sprinkle with parsley and serve.

Chicken with Celery

Photo, top

Refreshing celery and mild chicken harmonize well in this dish. Serve with rice or noodles.

4 servings
¹/₂ frying chicken (about 1¹/₄ to 1¹/₂ pounds/600 to 700 g), boned
10 ounces (300 g) trimmed celery
1 small onion
¹/₄ cup (60 g) butter
1 can (13 ounces/400 g) button mushrooms
¹/₂ teaspoon salt
Freshly ground pepper
Ground ginger
1 to 2 tablespoons fresh lemon juice
1 cup (240 mL) chicken stock
¹/₄ cup (60 mL) heavy cream

Cut chicken meat into cubes. Cut celery into pieces 1¹/₄ to 1¹/₂ inches (3 to 4 cm) long; halve lengthwise if very thick. Peel and mince onion. Melt butter in large saucepan, add onion, and sauté briefly. Add chicken and stir over high heat until white on all sides. Add celery and liquid from mushrooms. Season with salt, pepper, ginger, and lemon juice. Pour in chicken stock and simmer over medium-low heat 15 to 20 minutes. Add mushrooms and cream and cook over low heat 5 minutes. Serve immediately.

THE ONION FAMILY

Leeks

Like the other members of the onion family, leeks are a year-round kitchen staple. In summer, leeks tend to have a long white stalk, light green leaves, and a relatively mild flavor. Winter and spring leeks have a thicker, shorter white part, darker green leaves and a stronger taste. When the leeks are to be used as a seasoning, judge the amount you use accordingly; when they are the main ingredient, summer leeks are usually the best choice owing to their more delicate taste and texture. When braised in butter and lightly seasoned, leeks are a great side dish for nearly any meat or fish entrée. But the vegetable also lends itself well to gratinéeing with a béchamel or Mornay sauce; the cheese-flavored topping harmonizes beautifully with the flavor of leeks.

The following sauce is ideal for topping many vegetables: Celery, fennel, broccoli, Brussels sprouts, and so on are delicious when topped with béchamel, sprinkled with cheese, and slipped under the broiler until golden.

Béchamel Sauce

4 servings (makes about 2 1/2 cups/ 600 mL)
1 1/2 tablespoons (20 g) butter
2 tablespoons minced onion
3 1/2 tablespoons flour
3 cups (700 mL) degreased vegetable or chicken stock
1 cup (240 mL) heavy cream
1 teaspoon salt
pinch of freshly ground white pepper

Photo 1: Heat butter in saucepan over medium heat until foamy. Add onion and stir until translucent.

Photo 2: Sprinkle onion with flour and sauté briefly, stirring constantly; do not let mixture color.

Photo 3: Gradually pour in cold stock, whisking constantly to prevent lumps from forming.

Photo 4: Reduce heat to low and simmer sauce 30 minutes, stirring and skimming top occasionally. Meanwhile, pour cream into another saucepan and simmer briskly until reduced by half. Stir into sauce.

Photo 5: Line strainer with cheesecloth or muslin. Pour in sauce, gather corners of cloth together, and squeeze to press sauce through. Season with salt and pepper.

Leeks au Gratin

4 servings
6 to 8 leeks
Salt
Pinch of freshly grated nutmeg
Butter or margarine for baking dish
1 recipe Béchamel Sauce
3/4 cup (100 g) freshly grated cheese

Trim leeks and wash well. Drop into boiling salted water, add nutmeg, and cook until tender but not mushy, 10 to 15 minutes. Drain and plunge into ice water to stop cooking process. Drain well.

Photo 6: Grease flameproof baking dish or gratin pan with butter or margarine. Arrange drained leeks in dish. Pour sauce over and sprinkle with cheese. Bake in preheated 425°F (220°C) oven until cheese is lightly browned, 5 to 10 minutes. Serve immediately.

Onions

Depending on the type, onions are used both as seasoning and vegetable. The following recipe makes a perfect showcase for sweet, mild onions—here they are not just a flavoring but the main event.

Onion Casserole with Shrimp

Photo, bottom

4 servings
1 1/4 pounds (600 g) onions
Salt
1 clove garlic
7 slices (200 g) firm white bread
3 tablespoons (50 g) butter
1 tablespoon chopped fresh parsley
8 ounces (250 g) cooked shelled shrimp
3 ounces (80 g) boiled ham
1/2 cup (125 mL) milk
1/2 cup (125 mL) heavy cream
3 eggs
1/2 teaspoon salt
1 tablespoon chopped fresh parsley
Cayenne pepper or chopped fresh chili pepper

Peel onions. Drop into large pot of boiling salted water and cook 10 minutes, then lift out of water and drain well. Cut into slices about 3/8 inch (1 cm) thick. Peel and crush garlic. Dice bread. Melt butter in large skillet. Add garlic, bread cubes, and 1 tablespoon parsley and stir until bread is golden. Turn into large gratin dish and cover with half of onions. Top with shrimp, spacing evenly. Dice ham and sprinkle over shrimp, then cover with remaining onions.

Whisk milk, cream, and eggs together until smooth. Season with salt, 1 tablespoon parsley, and cayenne or chili pepper. Pour half of mixture over casserole and bake in preheated 400°F (200°C) oven for 15 minutes. Pour remaining milk mixture over and bake until set, about 20 minutes longer. Serve hot.

Stuffed Onions

Photo, top

Try serving these with freshly prepared tomato sauce (see recipe, page 58) and steamed rice.

4 servings
4 large onions, about 8 ounces (250 g) each
Salt
5 ounces (150 g) mixed ground meat
1 egg
2 tablespoons cooked rice
1 tablespoon chopped fresh parsley
1/2 clove garlic
3 tablespoons (40 g) butter
1/4 cup (60 mL) white wine

Peel onions. Drop into large pot of boiling salted water and cook 6 to 7 minutes. Lift onions out of water, drain well, and hollow out as thoroughly as possible with a sharp knife; mince onion removed from interiors. Peel and crush garlic. Mix chopped onion, meat, egg, rice, parsley, 1/4 teaspoon salt, and garlic and stuff onions with mixture (if there is any stuffing left over it can be cooked alongside the onions in the same pan).

Melt butter in large ovenproof skillet or flameproof baking dish and add onions. Pour wine over. Bake in preheated 400°F (200°C) oven until meat is cooked through, about 25 minutes.

ROOT AND BULB VEGETABLES

Beets

Though these deliciously earthy root vegetables are available all year round, their main season is the fall and winter. Purchase firm, round beets with taut skins. Be sure they still have an inch or so (2 to 3 cm) of green stalk, for if the stalks are cut completely away the beet's red color will bleed out during cooking.

Beets are always cooked in their skins; only after cooking are they peeled and otherwise prepared for the finished dish. First scrub them thoroughly under running water and cut away long stems and leaves to about 1 inch (2 to 3 cm) from the root. Cook the beets in boiling salted water until tender all the way through, 1 to 2 hours depending on size; test for tenderness with a knitting needle or long knife. When fully cooked, plunge the beets into ice water, trim away the stem and root ends, and pull off skin, then proceed with the chosen recipe.

Beets in Butter Sauce

Photo, bottom

A perfect side dish for meat, poultry or game.

4 to 6 servings
1 1/2 pounds (750 g) cooked beets
1 lemon
1 orange
5 tablespoons (70 g) butter
1/2 teaspoon salt
Freshly ground pepper
Freshly grated nutmeg
2 teaspoons chopped fresh parsley

Peel beets; slice with crinkle cutter or sharp knife. Scrub lemon and orange under hot running water. Peel colored part of skins very thinly with vegetable peeler, then cut into fine julienne (or use grater or zester to make very thin strips of peel). Squeeze juice from lemon and orange. Melt butter in saucepan. Add citrus peel and juice with beet slices and heat through, being careful not to overcook beets. Season with salt, pepper, nutmeg, and parsley and cook over very low heat for 5 to 10 minutes to blend flavors.

Bavarian-style Beets

Photo, top

The combination of beets and caraway is very popular in southern Germany and Austria.

4 servings
1 generous pound (500 g) freshly cooked beets
2 tablespoons wine vinegar
1/4 cup (60 mL) red wine
For the sauce
3 tablespoons (50 g) butter
1 tablespoon flour
1 1/2 cups (350 mL) meat stock
1 tablespoon wine vinegar
1/4 teaspoon salt
1/2 teaspoon sugar
1 teaspoon caraway seed

Peel beets, slice, and then cut into sticks. Place in non-aluminum bowl, add combined vinegar and wine, and toss to coat. Let marinate 30 minutes.

Meanwhile, melt butter in large saucepan, add flour, and stir briefly over medium-low heat. Pour in stock and simmer 8 to 10 minutes, stirring. Season sauce with vinegar, salt, sugar, and caraway. Drain beets and gently stir into sauce.

Variation

This dish is particularly delicious when 1/2 cup (125 mL) heavy cream is stirred in at the end; return the mixture to low heat just until heated through.

Salsify and Celery Root

After cooking, salsify somewhat resembles white asparagus. It is also called the "oyster plant" because it tastes quite a bit like oysters when cooked.

Salsify with Ham and Tomatoes

Photo, bottom

4 servings
2¼ pounds (1 kg) salsify (about 1¼ pounds after peeling and trimming)
Fresh lemon juice or vinegar
1 small onion
7 ounces (200 g) boiled ham
2 tablespoons vegetable oil
1 cup (240 mL) meat stock
¼ cup (60 mL) white wine
½ teaspoon salt
Freshly ground pepper
2 medium tomatoes
½ cup (125 mL) heavy cream
1 tablespoon chopped fresh parsley

Scrub salsify under running water; peel. To prevent discoloration, immediately drop into bowl of water acidulated with lemon juice or vinegar. Peel and chop onion. Dice ham. Heat oil in large saucepan, add onion, and sauté until tender. Add ham and sauté briefly. Cut salsify into pieces about 1¼ to 1½ inches (3 to 4 cm) long and add to saucepan. Pour meat stock and wine over, season with salt and pepper, and cook over medium heat 20 minutes. Meanwhile, blanch tomatoes briefly in boiling water, peel, and dice. Add to salsify with cream, reduce heat to low, and cook about 10 minutes longer. Sprinkle with parsley and serve.

Pan-fried Celery Root

Photo top

4 servings
1 celery root (about 2¼ pounds/1 kg)
Salt
Juice of 1 lemon
Flour
2 eggs
Breadcrumbs
6 tablespoons vegetable oil
⅓ cup (80 g) butter
For the remoulade
7 tablespoons (100 g) crème fraîche
3 tablespoons (50 g) mayonnaise
2 hard-cooked eggs
½ bell pepper
1 small onion
1 small pickle or cornichon
2 tablespoons chopped fresh herbs (chives, parsley, dill)
Salt and freshly ground pepper
Lemon wedges

Scrub celery root well under running water. Add lemon juice to large saucepan of boiling salted water, add celery root, and boil 20 to 25 minutes. Drain and let cool.

Peel celery root and cut into slices about ⅜ inch (1 cm) thick. Dredge slices in flour, dip into beaten egg, and coat with crumbs. Heat half the oil and half the butter in large skillet. Add celery root in batches and sauté on both sides until golden, adjusting heat as necessary and adding remaining oil and butter to skillet midway through cooking. Drain slices on paper towels and keep warm.

For the remoulade, combine crème fraîche and mayonnaise. Finely dice eggs, bell pepper, peeled onion, and pickle. Add to sauce with herbs and mix well. Season to taste with salt and pepper.

Serve celery root hot with lemon wedges and remoulade.

Carrots

A year-round staple, carrots are especially good in the summer, when they are fresh and tender. Appearance varies slightly by season; carrots are typically shorter and rounder in the spring, longer in winter.

Carrot Bouillon

Photo, bottom

4 servings
8 ounces (250 g) carrots
3 tablespoons vegetable oil
1 quart (1L) meat stock
Salt
Sugar
Freshly ground pepper
1/2 teaspoon chopped fresh parsley
1/2 teaspoon chopped fresh basil (preferably purple or opal basil)

Wash and peel carrots; cut into 1/4-inch (1/2-cm) slices with crinkle cutter. Heat oil in large saucepan, add carrot slices, and sauté for a few minutes over medium heat; do not brown. Pour in stock and simmer 20 to 25 minutes. Season with salt, sugar, and pepper. Ladle into bowls, sprinkle with chopped herbs, and serve.

Carrot Soup with Sour Cream

Photo, center

4 servings
1 generous pound (500 g) small carrots
1 small onion
1/2 large clove garlic
3 tablespoons (40 g) butter
1 quart (1 L) meat stock
1 teaspoon salt
Freshly ground pepper
1 teaspoon sweet paprika
1/2 cup (1/8 L) sour cream
1 tablespoon chopped fresh parsley

Wash and peel carrots; slice as thinly as possible. Peel and chop onion; peel and crush garlic. Melt butter in large saucepan, add onion and garlic and sauté until tender. Add carrot slices and cook over medium heat 10 minutes. Pour in meat stock. Season with salt, pepper and paprika and simmer for about 20 minutes. Strain soup through fine sieve. Whisk in sour cream and ladle into bowls. Sprinkle with parsley and serve.

Carrot One-pot

Photo, top

4 servings
1 generous pound (500 g) carrots
3 strips (100 g) bacon
2 tablespoons vegetable oil
1 small zucchini
2 medium tomatoes
1/2 cup (1/8 L) meat stock
1 teaspoon salt
Freshly ground pepper
Grated Emmenthal cheese (optional)

Wash, peel, and thinly slice carrots. Peel and finely chop onion; peel and crush garlic. Dice bacon. Heat oil in a large saucepan. Add onion, garlic, and diced bacon and sauté until translucent. Add carrot slices and cook over medium heat 10 minutes. Slice zucchini; dice tomatoes. Add to saucepan with meat stock and simmer for 15 to 20 minutes. Sprinkle with grated cheese, if desired, and serve.

CUCUMBERS AND SQUASH

Cucumbers and Winter Squash

An ancient vegetable, the cucumber apparently originated in India and came to Europe via Egypt and Rome. Today it is popular all over the world. Regular cucumbers no longer have a "season"; since they are grown in hothouses, they are available in equal abundance year round. Though usually thought of as a vegetable to be eaten raw in salads, they are also good when served as a hot side dish.

Though selective breeding has done away with bitterness, unfortunately it has also tended to weaken the typical cucumber flavor. But in late summer the markets offer short, thick pickling cucumbers, which have a wonderfully fresh and pronounced taste and are an excellent substitute for regular salad cucumbers in any recipe. Note that the pickling type, also known as Kirby cucumbers, should be peeled for they have a rather tough skin.

The various winter squashes are also ancient, and whether they originated in Africa or the Americas is still disputed by scholars. The squash family is enormous, but most of its members have similar flavor and yellow to orange flesh and can be prepared in more or less the same ways. Though so-called winter squash is becoming a year-round vegetable, it is cheapest and most abundant from September through the winter months.

Tomato-braised Cucumbers

Photo, bottom

4 servings
2¹/₄ pounds (1 kg) small pickling cucumbers
2 strips (50 g) bacon
1 medium onion
¹/₂ cup (125 mL) meat stock
¹/₂ teaspoon salt
Freshly ground pepper
1 teaspoon sweet paprika
2 medium tomatoes
1 tablespoon chopped fresh dill
3 tablespoons sour cream

Peel cucumbers and trim ends, which often have a bitter taste. Halve cucumbers lengthwise and scrape out seeds with a teaspoon. Cut flesh into strips about 1¹/₄ inches (3 cm) long and ³/₈ inch (1 cm) wide. Dice bacon. Peel onion and cut into quarters or eighths. Sauté bacon in saucepan until fat is rendered. Add onion and sauté until translucent. Add meat stock, cucumber, salt, pepper, and paprika and simmer 15 minutes. Blanch tomatoes briefly in boiling water; peel and cut into eighths. Add to cucumber mixture and cook 5 minutes longer. Stir in dill and sour cream and serve.

Creamy Winter Squash

Photo, top

Delicious with meat or poultry.

4 servings
2¹/₄ pounds (1 kg) peeled and trimmed winter squash, such as butternut
Juice of 1 lemon
1 teaspoon salt
2 strips (60 g) bacon
1 small onion
¹/₂ teaspoon sugar
Freshly ground pepper
1 cup (240 mL) meat stock
2 tablespoons chopped fresh dill
¹/₂ cup (125 mL) crème fraîche

Cut squash into ¹/₂-inch (1¹/₂-cm) cubes. Place in bowl and sprinkle with lemon juice and salt. Finely dice bacon. Peel and finely chop onion. Place bacon in saucepan and sauté over moderate heat until fat is rendered. Add onion and sauté until tender. Add squash, sprinkle with sugar and pepper, and pour in meat stock. Simmer uncovered until squash is tender and liquid is nearly evaporated, about 15 to 20 minutes. Stir in dill and crème fraîche and heat through.

Zucchini

Like other summer squash, zucchini is picked while still immature; consequently, its skin is thin and tender and the seeds are tiny and undeveloped. It is an extremely versatile vegetable that lends itself to many preparations. Though available year round, summer and fall zucchini is usually of the highest quality.

Stuffed Zucchini

Serve with fresh tomato sauce (see recipe, page 58).

4 servings
4 zucchini (about 7 ounces/ 200 g each)
1 medium onion
1/2 clove garlic
1 tablespoon olive oil
1 generous pound (500 g) mixed ground meat
5 ounces (150 g) Swiss or Emmenthal cheese
1 teaspoon salt
Freshly ground pepper
1 teaspoon sweet paprika
2 eggs
1 tablespoon chopped fresh basil
1/2 teaspoon dried thyme
1/4 cup breadcrumbs
5 tablespoons (75 g) butter

Wash zucchini well and trim ends; halve lengthwise. Peel and mince onion; peel and crush garlic. Heat olive oil in skillet, add onion and garlic, and sauté until tender. Place meat in large mixing bowl. Add finely diced cheese, onion mixture, salt, pepper, paprika, eggs, basil, and thyme and blend to form a soft stuffing. Divide among zucchini halves. Sprinkle with breadcrumbs and drizzle with 3 tablespoons (50 g) melted butter. Arrange in greased baking dish and bake in preheated 400°F (200°C) oven until cooked through, about 20 to 25 minutes.

Tomato-zucchini Casserole

Photo on page 2

4 servings
2 small zucchini
2 medium tomatoes
1 small onion
12 ounces (400 g) mixed ground meat
1 3/4 cups (100 g) cooked white rice
1/2 teaspoon salt
1 tablespoon chopped fresh basil
Freshly ground pepper
1 egg
1/3 cup (80 g) butter
1/2 cup (60 g) freshly grated Parmesan cheese

Wash, dry, and slice zucchini and tomatoes. Peel and chop onion. Combine meat, onion, rice, seasonings, and egg. Grease medium baking dish with about 2 tablespoons (25 g) butter. Arrange a layer of tomato and zucchini slices in bottom of dish. Spread with meat mixture; cover with remaining vegetable slices. Bake in preheated 400°F (200°C) oven for 20 minutes. Sprinkle with cheese, dot with remaining butter, and bake 20 minutes longer. Serve hot.

SWEET CORN

Though it is a native American favorite, corn has been cultivated in Italy since the 17th century and from there has spread all over Europe.

Corn Fritters

Photo, bottom

4 servings
1/2 cup (125 mL) milk
2 eggs
2 tablespoons flour
1/2 teaspoon salt
Freshly ground pepper
4 ears of corn

Whisk milk, egg, and flour to form smooth batter; season with salt and pepper. Using sharp knife, scrape corn kernels from cob starting at stem end. Stir corn into batter. Heat butter or oil in small skillet. Drop 1 heaping tablespoon batter into skillet and spread gently. Fry, turning once, until golden brown on both sides.

Corn Casserole

Photo, top

4 servings
5 ears of corn
2 cups (450 mL) meat stock
1 small onion
2 medium tomatoes
5 ounces (150 g) boiled ham
1 red bell pepper
3 tablespoons (40 g) butter
1/2 teaspoon salt
2 teaspoons Tabasco sauce
10 black olives
2 eggs
3/4 cup (100 g) grated Emmenthal cheese
2 tablespoons breadcrumbs
3 tablespoons (40 g) butter, cut into small pieces

Scrape corn kernels from cob as in preceding recipe. Drop kernels into boiling meat stock and simmer 5 to 6 minutes, then drain well. Peel and chop onion. Remove stem ends from tomatoes; coarsely dice tomatoes with skin and seeds. Dice them. Stem, seed, and dice bell pepper. Melt butter in skillet, add onion, and sauté until translucent. Add tomato, ham, and bell pepper, season with salt and Tabasco, and cook 5 minutes. Mix in half of corn. Butter baking dish and spread with tomato mixture. Pit and dice olives. Mix remaining corn with eggs, cheese, and olives and spread as second layer atop mixture in baking dish. Sprinkle with breadcrumbs and dot with butter. Bake in preheated 400°F (200°C) oven until top is golden, about 30 to 40 minutes.

THE VERSATILE EGGPLANT

Eggplant originated in Southeast Asia. Today specialty produce markets carry eggplants of various shapes and colors, but the typical globe eggplant is available year round in every supermarket.

Imam Bayildi

Photo, bottom

4 servings
4 small eggplants
3 small onions
1 generous pound (500 g) tomatoes
2 cloves garlic
5 tablespoons olive oil
1 bay leaf
1 tablespoon chopped fresh parsley
1 teaspoon salt
Pinch of sugar
1 cinnamon stick
1/2 cup (50 g) chopped almonds

Roast eggplants in preheated 400°F (200°C) oven for 15 minutes, turning frequently. Halve lengthwise and scoop out interior, leaving 3/4-inch (2-cm) shell. Finely chop flesh removed from eggplants. Peel and thinly slice onions. Blanch tomatoes briefly in boiling water; peel and chop finely. Peel garlic and force through garlic press. Heat half of oil in skillet, add onion, and sauté until tender. Add tomato and garlic, cover, and braise for 5 minutes. Add seasonings and chopped eggplant and cook 10 minutes. Discard bay leaf and cinnamon stick and stir in almonds.

Arrange eggplant halves in oiled baking dish and fill with stuffing mixture. Sprinkle with remaining oil. Bake in preheated 350°F (180°C) oven for 15 to 20 minutes.

Turkish Eggplant Skillet

Photo, top

4 servings
1 generous pound (500 g) eggplant
Salt
3 small onions
1 clove garlic
3 tomatoes
1 1/2 pounds (750 g) lamb shoulder or shank
3 tablespoons (45 g) butter
3 tablespoons olive oil
Coarsely ground pepper
2 cups (450 mL) hot meat stock
1 tablespoon chopped fresh parsley

Wash eggplant and trim stem end. Cut eggplant into cubes. Toss in large bowl with 1 tablespoon salt and let stand 30 minutes to draw out bitter juices. Peel and chop onion; peel and crush garlic. Blanch tomatoes briefly in boiling water; peel and cut into pieces. Cut lamb into cubes. Melt butter and oil in large skillet with tight-fitting lid. Rinse eggplant cubes and pat dry. Add to skillet and sauté until lightly browned on all sides, then remove and drain on paper towels. Add lamb to fat remaining in skillet and brown on all sides over high heat; remove and set aside. Sauté onion in skillet until golden brown. Add tomato and garlic and simmer 5 minutes, then return lamb to skillet. Season with 1 teaspoon salt and pepper, pour in meat stock, cover, and simmer over low heat 30 minutes. Add eggplant and simmer 30 minutes longer. Sprinkle with parsley and serve.

Stuffed Eggplant

Photo, bottom

4 servings
4 small eggplants
1 small onion
1 clove garlic
1/2 bell pepper
8 ounces boneless lamb
1 medium tomato
1/2 cup (125 mL) olive oil
1/2 teaspoon salt
2 teaspoons sweet paprika
Pinch of ground cumin
Pinch of ground allspice
Pinch of cayenne pepper
Butter for baking dish
1 cup (240 mL) meat stock

Wash and dry eggplants; trim stem ends. Using paring knife, make lengthwise slits in eggplant about 3/8 inch (1 cm) apart, then peel away alternating strips of skin between slits. Pierce peeled areas several times with point of knife to promote even cooking. Peel and mince onion; peel and crush garlic. Dice bell pepper; mince or grind lamb. Blanch tomato briefly in boiling water; peel and crush. Heat oil in large skillet, add eggplants, and sauté on all sides. Transfer 2 tablespoons oil to another skillet, add onion and garlic, and sauté until tender.

Add bell pepper and sauté briefly. Stir in lamb and brown over high heat 2 to 3 minutes. Add tomato, salt, and remaining seasonings. Make deep lengthwise cut into each eggplant and gently spread open. Fill with stuffing mixture. Butter baking dish. Arrange stuffed eggplants in dish, pour in meat stock, and bake in preheated 400°F (200°C) oven for 20 minutes.

Eggplant-tomato Casserole

Photo, top

4 servings
1 1/2 pounds (750 g) eggplant
3 tablespoons vegetable oil
1 1/2 cups (350 mL) chicken stock
1 teaspoon salt
Freshly ground pepper
1 dinner roll
1 small onion
2 tablespoons (30 g) butter
1 tablespoon chopped fresh parsley
1 teaspoon dried oregano
4 tomatoes
3 ounces (80 g) Emmenthal cheese
1/4 cup (30 g) freshly grated Parmesan cheese

Peel eggplant and cut into slices about 3/8 inch (1 cm) thick. Heat oil in large shallow saucepan or deep skillet. Add eggplant slices and 1 cup (240 mL) chicken stock, season with salt and pepper, and simmer until tender, 10 to 12 minutes. Remove eggplant, drain, and puree in blender or processor. Thinly slice roll and soften in remaining 1/2 cup (125 mL) chicken stock. Peel and mince onion. Melt butter in skillet, add onion, and sauté until tender. Add roll, parsley, and oregano, then blend this mixture into eggplant puree. Slice tomatoes. Layer half of tomato slices in baking dish and spread with eggplant mixture. Cover with a second layer of remaining tomatoes. Bake in preheated 400°F (200°C) oven 20 minutes. Finely dice Emmenthal cheese, mix with Parmesan, and sprinkle over casserole. Bake until light golden, about 20 minutes longer, and serve.

TOMATOES AND BELL PEPPERS

Tomatoes

If flavor is of any value to you, always buy outdoor-grown, not hothouse, tomatoes. This confines you largely to the growing season; even with modern transport, tomatoes remain a seasonal treat that is at its best from April to October.

Spinach-stuffed Tomatoes

Photo, bottom

4 servings
12 ounces fresh young spinach
1 small onion
3 tablespoons (50 g) butter or margarine
3 tablespoons heavy cream
1/3 cup (40 g) chopped walnuts
Salt
Pinch of freshly grated nutmeg
4 small tomatoes
Salt and freshly ground pepper
Butter for baking dish
1/2 cup (50 g) shredded mixed Parmesan and Emmenthal cheese
3 tablespoons (50 g) butter

Pick over, stem, and thoroughly wash spinach. Place in large saucepan with water clinging to leaves and stir over medium heat for 10 minutes. Transfer to sieve and drain well. Peel and finely chop onion. Melt butter or margarine in skillet, add onion, and sauté until tender. Coarsely chop spinach, add to onion, and heat through briefly. Stir in cream and walnuts; season with salt and nutmeg.

Wash tomatoes and cut off top third. Hollow out centers. Season with salt and pepper and stuff with spinach mixture. Butter shallow baking dish. Arrange tomatoes in dish, sprinkle with cheese and dot with butter. Bake in preheated 400°F (200°C) oven until cheese is melted, about 15 minutes. Serve hot.

Stuffed Tomatoes Provençale

Photo, top

Good with practically any meat entrée, and with fish dishes that would benefit by a garlic-scented accompaniment.

4 servings
4 medium tomatoes
3 tablespoons vegetable oil
1 shallot
2 tablespoons chopped fresh parsley
1 tablespoon chopped fresh basil
1 teaspoon chopped fresh sage
A few rosemary leaves
2 cloves garlic
1/4 teaspoon salt
Freshly ground pepper
2 tablespoons breadcrumbs
3 tablespoons (50 g) butter

Wash and stem tomatoes; halve horizontally. Brush ovenproof skillet or baking dish with the oil and arrange tomatoes in skillet cut side up. Peel and mince shallot; combine with herbs. Peel and crush garlic and add to herb mixture with salt, pepper, and breadcrumbs. Divide among cut sides of tomatoes, hollowing tomatoes slightly if necessary. Dot with butter. Bake in preheated 425°F (220°C) oven until crumbs are golden, about 12 to 15 minutes.

Pepper-tomato Skillet

Few vegetables go together as well as tomatoes and peppers. This spicy mixture is delicious topped with fried eggs.

4 servings
1 medium onion
2 cloves garlic
2 tablespoons olive oil
3 green or red bell peppers
4 ounces (120 g) boiled ham
2 large tomatoes
1 teaspoon salt
Freshly ground pepper
1 teaspoon sweet paprika
1 tablespoon chopped fresh parsley
1 teaspoon dried oregano
2 tablespoons breadcrumbs
5 ounces (150 g) frozen peas
7 ounces (200 g) smoked sausage

Peel and finely dice onion. Peel and crush garlic. Wash and seed bell peppers; dice flesh. Cut ham into similar-size dice. Heat oil in large skillet. Add onion and garlic and sauté until tender. Add bell pepper and ham and sauté over high heat 5 to 6 minutes. Blanch tomatoes briefly in boiling water, peel off skin, and dice flesh; add to skillet. Season with salt, pepper, paprika, parsley, and oregano and simmer 10 minutes. Stir in breadcrumbs and then peas. Butter baking dish; add mixture to dish, spreading evenly. Slice sausage and mix in, or arrange on top of tomato mixture. Bake in preheated 400°F (200°C) oven 15 to 20 minutes.

Hungarian-style Tomatoes and Peppers

Not illustrated

This is as simple as it is tasty.

4 servings
1 generous pound (500 g) tomatoes
2 large green bell peppers
3 strips (80 g) bacon
2 tablespoons (25 g) butter
1 medium onion
1 teaspoon salt
1/2 cup (125 mL) full-bodied red wine
2 tablespoons sour cream

Wash, stem, and dice tomatoes. Wash, stem, and seed peppers: cut into large pieces. Finely dice bacon. Peel and chop onion. Melt butter in large saucepan, add bacon, and sauté until fat is rendered. Add onion and sauté until tender. Mix in tomato and pepper pieces, salt, and red wine. Cover and simmer 20 to 30 minutes. Stir in sour cream and serve.

Bell Peppers

These days green, red, and yellow bell peppers are all widely available. The green ones are usually cheapest and are sold year round; the milder, sweeter red and yellow peppers are in season from August to October.

Meat-stuffed Peppers

Photo, bottom

For a special touch, top each pepper with a dollop of sour cream just before serving. Rice or boiled potatoes make a good accompaniment.

4 servings
4 yellow bell peppers
1 small onion
1/2 clove garlic
8 ounces (250 g) mixed ground meat
1 tablespoon chopped fresh parsley
1/2 teaspoon salt
Freshly ground pepper
2 eggs
Sour cream (optional)

For the tomato sauce
1 small onion
1 generous pound (500 g) very ripe tomatoes
3 tablespoons vegetable oil
1/2 cup (125 mL) meat stock
1/2 teaspoon sugar
1/2 teaspoon salt
Freshly ground pepper
1 teaspoon chopped fresh basil

Wash peppers and cut off tops; carefully remove stems and white membranes. Peel and mince onion. Peel and crush garlic. Combine meat, onion, garlic, parsley, salt, and pepper and blend well by hand, then mix in egg. Divide among peppers, pressing stuffing in well. Cover with pepper tops. Butter baking dish and arrange peppers in dish.

For the sauce, peel and chop onion; dice tomatoes. Heat oil in large saucepan, add onion, and sauté until translucent but not colored. Add tomato, meat stock, sugar, salt, pepper, and basil and simmer uncovered 15 to 20 minutes. Meanwhile, bake peppers in preheated 400°F (200°C) oven 15 minutes. Strain sauce and pour over peppers. Bake 20 to 25 minutes longer.

Cheese-stuffed Peppers

Photo, top

Crusty French or Italian bread is the best partner for this simple but marvelously flavorful dish.

4 servings
4 red bell peppers
5 ounces (150 g) feta cheese
1 egg
Sour cream (optional)
1/2 teaspoon salt
1/4 cup (60 mL) vegetable oil

Wash and dry peppers. Arrange side by side on baking sheet and roast in preheated 400°F (200°C) oven until flesh has collapsed and skin is dark brown on all sides. Transfer to plastic bag or covered container for 10 minutes. Peel and cut open lengthwise; remove seeds and membranes. Mash cheese with fork and blend in egg (mixture should be thick and creamy; if still dry, mix in sour cream as necessary). Stuff peppers with cheese mixture and fold closed. Arrange in buttered baking dish cut side up; sprinkle with salt and drizzle with oil. Bake in preheated 350°F (180°C) oven 30 to 40 minutes.

THE DELICIOUS POTATO

Though potatoes are among Americans' favorite foods, we seldom think of them as a "vegetable"—though, like other vegetables, they are rich in minerals, vitamins, and fiber and quite low in calories.

Be sure to buy potatoes of good quality—which means ignoring the ones sold in plastic bags. Avoid those with soft or green spots or, of course, with sprouting eyes; good potatoes are firm and crisp to the touch, without wrinkles or bruises. Store them in a cool, airy place.

Stuffed Soufflé Potatoes

A delectable complement to meat or fish.

6 servings
6 small baking potatoes
2 tablespoons (30 g) butter
2 eggs, separated
3 tablespoons heavy cream
1/2 teaspoon salt
Freshly ground pepper
Freshly grated nutmeg

Scrub potatoes well under running water. Cut 6 pieces of aluminum foil large enough to wrap around potatoes. Brush foil with vegetable oil and wrap each potato tightly. Bake on middle rack of preheated 425°F (220°C) oven 45 minutes.

Unwrap potatoes and let cool. Cut away about 1/4 of potato from one side and hollow out potato with spoon (preferably a grapefruit spoon), leaving a 3/8-inch (1-cm) shell. Cut butter into small pieces and divide among potatoes. Force scooped-out flesh through fine sieve; add egg yolks, cream, salt, pepper, and nutmeg and blend until smooth and creamy. Beat egg whites to stiff peaks and fold into potato mixture. Stuff into potato shells. Arrange in buttered baking dish and bake in preheated 425°F (220°C) oven until top is browned and crusty.

Potatoes with Bacon

Not illustrated

4 servings
2 1/4 pounds (1 kg) boiling potatoes
6 strips (120 g) bacon
1 small onion
1 teaspoon salt
Freshly ground pepper
1 cup (120 g) grated Emmenthal cheese (optional)
1 tablespoon minced fresh chives

Peel potatoes and slice as thinly as possible on mandoline. Finely dice bacon. Peel and finely dice onion. Sauté bacon in skillet until fat is rendered, removing bacon bits with slotted spoon before they are browned. Add onion to bacon fat in skillet and sauté until tender. Add potatoes, season with salt and pepper, cover, and cook 10 to 15 minutes without stirring. Uncover and turn potatoes browned side up. Add bacon bits and cook, stirring frequently, until potatoes are crisp and brown. If desired, top with cheese, cover skillet, and heat until cheese is melted. Sprinkle with chives and serve.

Mediterranean Potato Casserole

Serve with cold beer and a crisp green salad.

4 servings
1³/₄ pounds (800 g) uniform-size boiling potatoes
1 generous pound (500 g) tomatoes
4 hard-cooked eggs
1 can anchovy fillets
1 teaspoon salt
¹/₄ teaspoon freshly ground pepper
1 cup (240 mL) sour cream
1 tablespoon chopped fresh parsley
1 tablespoon minced fresh chives

Boil potatoes in their jackets until tender. Drain, cool, and slice. Wash, dry, and slice tomatoes. Shell and slice eggs. Drain anchovies well on paper towels. Generously grease baking dish. Layer potato, tomato, and egg slices in dish, seasoning with salt and pepper and inserting anchovy fillets at intervals. Whisk sour cream with herbs and pour over top of casserole. Bake in preheated 400°F (200°C) oven 30 to 40 minutes.

Potato Goulash

Not illustrated

In Hungary this is often prepared without meat, in which case it is known as potatoes *paprikásh*. With the addition of pork it becomes a delicious entrée. For a gravylike sauce, use boiling potatoes that stay firm after cooking; for a thicker, creamier sauce, use baking potatoes.

4 servings
1³/₄ pounds (800 g) potatoes
1 teaspoon salt
1 small onion
1 medium carrot
¹/₂ parsley root
1 leek
3 tablespoons (50 g) butter
1 rounded tablespoon sweet paprika
12 ounces (400 g) boneless pork shoulder
3 cups (700 mL) meat stock
¹/₂ cup (125 mL) sour cream
1 tablespoon chopped fresh parsley

Peel potatoes and cut into ⁵/₈-inch (1¹/₂-cm) cubes. Place in large bowl and sprinkle with the salt. Peel and chop onion. Clean carrot, parsley root, and leek; finely dice carrot and parsley root and thinly slice leek. Melt butter in large saucepan, add onion, and sauté until tender. Add carrot, parsley root, and leek to saucepan, sprinkle with paprika, and sauté over medium-high heat 3 to 4 minutes. Cut meat into cubes, add to saucepan, and brown on all sides for 5 to 6 minutes. Stir in potato and meat stock, cover, and simmer over medium heat 15 minutes, stirring occasionally and testing meat and potatoes for doneness toward end of cooking time; add more stock or water if liquid evaporates. Stir in sour cream and let stand off heat or over low heat for a few minutes to blend flavors. Sprinkle with parsley and serve.

COLORFUL VEGETABLE MIXTURES

Ratatouille

This classic dish originated in Nice.

4 servings
2 small eggplants (about 1 pound/450 to 500 g)
3 small zucchini (about 8 ounces/250 g)
2 medium tomatoes (about 8 ounces/250 g)
1 red bell pepper
1 green bell pepper
1 small onion
2 cloves garlic
5 tablespoons olive oil
2 to 3 celery stalks, cleaned
1/2 cup (125 mL) white wine
1 bay leaf
1 teaspoon chopped fresh thyme
2 teaspoons chopped fresh parsley
Freshly ground pepper
1 teaspoon salt
1 cup (240 mL) meat stock

Wash and trim eggplants and zucchini. Cut unpeeled eggplant into 3/4-inch (2-cm) cubes; thinly slice zucchini. Blanch tomatoes briefly in boiling water; peel, stem, and cut into large cubes. Halve bell peppers and discard stems and seeds; cut into small cubes. Peel and chop onion; peel and crush garlic. Heat olive oil in large saucepan. Add onion and garlic and sauté until translucent. Mince celery; add to saucepan with wine, bay leaf, thyme, parsley, pepper, and salt and cook 3 to 4 minutes. Add eggplant, zucchini, tomato, and bell peppers with meat stock. Cover and simmer over very low heat 1 hour, then uncover and cook about 25 minutes longer to thicken.

Italian Vegetable One-pot

Photo on cover

In contrast to ratatouille, in which the vegetables are cooked until very tender, the vegetables here should be crisp-tender or *al dente*.

4 servings
2 medium onions
1 clove garlic
1/4 cup olive oil
1 teaspoon chopped chili pepper
2 cups (450 mL) meat stock
2 medium eggplants
2 medium zucchini
2 yellow bell peppers
1 1/2 red bell peppers
10 ounces (300 g) young green beans
1 teaspoon salt
Freshly ground pepper
2 tablespoons chopped mixed fresh herbs (parsley, sage, thyme, rosemary, and lemon balm)

Peel and thinly slice onions; peel and crush garlic. Heat oil in large saucepan. Add onions, garlic, and minced chili pepper and sauté briefly. Pour in meat stock and cook uncovered over medium heat until liquid is reduced by half. Wash and trim eggplants and zucchini; cut eggplants into pieces and slice zucchini. Stem and seed bell peppers and cut into strips. Trim ends of beans; if beans are large, cut in half. Add vegetables to saucepan in order listed and cook each 1 to 2 minutes before adding the next. Season with salt, pepper, and herbs and cook uncovered over medium-high heat, stirring frequently, until cooked to desired tenderness, about 20 to 25 minutes.

GRILLED AND FRIED

Grilled Vegetables

Grilling is an ideal cooking method for many types of vegetables, for the strong, dry heat of a barbecue or broiler makes the outside of the vegetables browned and crisp while the inside stays moist. Among those vegetables that lend themselves especially well to grilling are zucchini, eggplant, tomatoes, bell peppers, corn, large mushrooms, onions, artichokes, fennel, and potatoes. Grilling over charcoal makes for wonderful flavor, particularly if you add herb sprigs—for example, rosemary, thyme, oregano, or a few bay leaves—to the coals.

Whether you use an indoor or outdoor grill, the vegetables must be prepared beforehand. Large ones should be cut into smaller pieces so that the inside cooks evenly before the outside becomes overcooked or charred. The vegetables should be brushed generously with oil (to prevent them from sticking to the grill) and seasoned with herbs, pepper, and salt. Alternatively, they can be marinated for 30 minutes or so before cooking, using a well-seasoned marinade containing plenty of chopped fresh herbs as well as salt, pepper, and perhaps some garlic. Take care to turn the vegetables frequently during grilling to promote even cooking.

Artichokes: Miniature artichokes are excellent for grilling. Halve lengthwise and sprinkle with lemon juice, then brush with oil. Grill the cut sides first.

Bell peppers: To retain juices, grill the peppers whole, then cut open, remove seeds, and sprinkle with seasonings after cooking.

Corn on the cob: Either wrap with several strips of bacon and secure with toothpicks or brush with oil, sprinkle with seasonings, and wrap in aluminum foil. Corn will dry out rapidly if grilled unprotected.

Eggplant: Small eggplants are best for grilling. Halve lengthwise; if using larger eggplant, slash several times with a knife to help heat penetrate.

Fennel: Use the smallest bulbs available; halve lengthwise. Always blanch fennel in a large pot of boiling water for 5 minutes before grilling.

Mushrooms: The best mushrooms for grilling are those with very large caps. Cut in half and grill the cut sides first.

Onions: Use mild onions for grilling; cut in quarters or sixths.

Potatoes: Use mealy baking potatoes of uniform size. Scrub well, cut a deep cross into each potato, and wrap individually in oiled aluminum foil. Lay directly in the embers and cook until easily pierced with a wooden skewer.

Tomatoes: Small tomatoes can be grilled whole; large ones should be halved and the cut sides grilled first.

Zucchini: Halve small zucchini lengthwise; cut large ones (as in photo) into slices about 3/8 inch (1 cm) thick.

Deep-fried Vegetables

The technique of deep-frying in batter is well suited to many vegetables, for in the crisp, protective batter coating the vegetable's own flavor is perfectly preserved. Especially good for deep-frying are mushrooms of various kinds, Brussels sprouts, broccoli, zucchini, eggplant, artichokes, beans, and small onions. Vegetables requiring longer cooking times should be blanched before frying so that they will be fully cooked after the relatively short frying time. Flavors will come out best if the vegetable is seasoned only lightly before coating with batter.

The following recipe, in which the vegetable is marinated in a piquant oil mixture before frying, makes a very good main course. Serve with two or three cold sauces—perhaps aïoli, a yogurt-herb sauce, and mayonnaise seasoned to taste. French bread is a good accompaniment.

4 servings
2 small zucchini
2 ounces (250 g) fresh mushrooms
8 ounces (250 g) cauliflower (weighed after trimming)
8 ounces (250 g) green beans
Salt

8 to 10 bacon slices
1 cup (240 mL) vegetable or olive oil
3 tablespoons chopped mixed fresh herbs (parsley, chives, basil, thyme, and a little rosemary)
1 small onion
1 clove garlic
Freshly ground pepper
Vegetable oil for frying
For the batter
2 cups (240 g) flour
4 egg yolks
3 tablespoons (40 g) butter, melted and warm
1/2 teaspoon salt
1 1/2 cups (350 mL) beer
3 egg whites

Photo 1: Place flour for batter in mixing bowl. Add egg yolks, butter, salt, and beer and whisk to form smooth batter. Cover and let stand at room temperature at least 1 hour.

Photo 2: Meanwhile, prepare vegetables. Wash and trim zucchini; cut into slices 1/4 inch (1/2 cm) thick. Clean and trim mushrooms. Divide cauliflower into florets. Trim green beans. Blanch cauliflower and beans separately in large pot of boiling salted water for 3 to 4 minutes; drain well. Wrap beans into small bundles with bacon slices and secure with toothpicks. Peel and finely chop onion; peel and crush garlic.

Combine oil, herbs, onion, garlic, pepper, and 1/2 teaspoon salt in mixing bowl. Add vegetables and marinate 1 hour.

Photo 3: Heat oil to 350°F (180°C) in large saucepan or deep-fryer. Beat egg whites to stiff peaks and gently fold into batter with whisk; at this point batter should be used without delay.

Photo 4: Using long two-pronged fork, spear vegetable pieces one at a time and drain briefly. Dip into batter, being careful to coat completely; let excess batter run off.

Photo 5: Place coated vegetables in hot fat a few at a time and fry until bottom is browned, then turn and fry second side.

Photo 6: After frying, the vegetables should be crisp and golden brown on all sides, tender and moist within. Drain on paper towels and serve immediately.

THE CABBAGE FAMILY

Savoy Cabbage

Savoy cabbage is available year round. The early varieties, sold through June or so, are usually light green, with loose, crinkled leaves. Later-season types vary from dark green to bluish green and have more compact leaves.

Stuffed Savoy Cabbage

Photo, bottom

4 servings
8 large Savoy cabbage leaves
Salt
1 small onion
1/2 clove garlic
12 ounces (350 g) mixed ground meat
1 teaspoon paprika
Freshly ground pepper
1 tablespoon chopped fresh parsley
1 egg
2 tablespoons (30 g) butter
1/2 cup (125 mL) white wine
1/2 cup (125 mL) meat stock

Blanch cabbage leaves in boiling salted water for 2 minutes, then drain and plunge into ice water to stop cooking process. Cut away coarse ribs. Lay 4 leaves on work surface and top each with another leaf. Peel and mince onion; peel and crush garlic. Combine meat, onion, garlic, paprika, 1/2 teaspoon salt, parsley, and egg. Divide mixture into 4 equal parts and set 1 portion on top of each pair of leaves. Roll up to enclose filling completely; tie each roll securely with cotton thread Melt butter in flameproof baking dish or ovenproof saucepan. Add roulades and sauté briefly over medium-high heat, turning several times. Pour in wine and meat stock. Bake in preheated 400°F (200°C) oven 20 to 25 minutes, turning rolls occasionally and covering with foil if they darken too quickly. Remove roulades with slotted spoon and keep warm. Boil cooking liquid on top of stove until thickened to desired sauce consistency and serve with cabbage rolls.

Creamed Savoy Cabbage Wedges

Photo, top

4 to 6 servings
1 head Savoy cabbage (2 to 2 1/2 pounds/1 to 1 1/4 kg)
Salt
3 tablespoons (40 g) butter
1/4 cup (30 g) flour
1 cup (240 mL) milk
1/2 teaspoon salt
Freshly ground pepper
Freshly grated nutmeg
1/2 cup (125 mL) heavy cream
6 slices (120 g) bacon
1 green onion
2 tablespoons (30 g) butter
1 tablespoon finely chopped fresh chives

Remove limp outer leaves from cabbage and cut deep cross in base of core. Cook cabbage in large pot of boiling salted water until tender throughout, about 10 to 15 minutes. Cut into quarters and drain well. Melt butter in medium saucepan. Add flour and stir several minutes over low heat. Pour in milk and cook 5 minutes, stirring constantly. Season with salt, pepper, and nutmeg and simmer sauce until thickened and creamy. Whip cream to soft peaks and fold into sauce. Finely dice bacon and cook in skillet over medium heat until fat is rendered; discard fat. Trim and finely chop green onion.

Melt butter in flameproof baking dish or ovenproof skillet. Add onion and sauté until tender. Add drained cabbage quarters, pour sauce over, and sprinkle with bacon bits. Bake in preheated 425°F (220°C) until sauce is lightly glazed, about 2 to 3 minutes. Sprinkle with chives and serve.

Broccoli

Though there are many types of broccoli—including a nearly white one and a purple variety that resembles cauliflower—regular green broccoli, with large florets topping thick, firm stalks, is virtually the only kind to be found in American markets. Its high season was traditionally from October to April, but broccoli has become a year-round vegetable.

Broccoli Pie

Photo, bottom

4 servings
1¹/₄ pounds (600 g) broccoli
2 medium shallots
¹/₂ clove garlic
3 tablespoons (40 g) butter
¹/₂ teaspoon salt
Freshly ground pepper
4 eggs
1 cup (240 mL) heavy cream
A few drops Tabasco sauce
Freshly grated nutmeg
¹/₂ teaspoon salt
¹/₃ cup (40 g) sliced almonds

Wash broccoli well under cold running water and trim ends of stalks. Divide top into small florets. Peel thick stalks and cut into pieces. Drain well in strainer or colander. Peel and mince shallot. Peel and crush garlic. Melt butter in flameproof 10-inch (24- to 26-cm) quiche dish. Add shallot and garlic and sauté until tender. Add broccoli, season with salt and pepper, and cook 5 minutes over low heat.

Meanwhile, whisk eggs with cream, Tabasco, nutmeg, and salt; pour over broccoli mixture. Bake in preheated 400°F (200°C) oven until custard is almost set, 50 to 55 minutes. Lightly toast almonds in ungreased small skillet. Sprinkle over pie and serve.

Savory Braised Broccoli

Photo, top

4 servings
1¹/₂ pounds (750 g) broccoli
¹/₄ cup (60 mL) vegetable oil
1 cup (240 mL) chicken stock
1 cup (240 mL) dry white wine
¹/₂ teaspoon salt
Freshly ground pepper
1 small onion
For the sauce (optional)
1 egg yolk
¹/₂ cup (125 mL) heavy cream

Wash broccoli. Peel thick stalks and cut into pieces; divide into small florets. Heat oil in large saucepan, add broccoli, and immediately pour in chicken stock and wine. Season with salt and pepper and add whole peeled onion. Braise broccoli over medium heat 10 to 15 minutes, testing frequently and removing from heat when crisp-tender; do not overcook. Lift out broccoli with slotted spoon and keep warm. Boil cooking liquid until reduced to about ¹/₂ cup (125 mL). If desired, whisk in egg yolk and cream and cook over low heat until slightly thickened. Pour sauce over broccoli and serve.

Cauliflower

Available all year, but particularly abundant in summer and fall.

Spanish Cauliflower

Photo, bottom

4 servings
1 cauliflower (about 1¹/₂ pounds/750 g)
Salt
3 hard-cooked eggs
1 clove garlic
¹/₄ cup (60 mL) olive oil
2 tablespoons chopped fresh parsley
2 tablespoons coarsely chopped pine nuts

Trim and wash cauliflower; divide into florets. Drop into large pot of boiling salted water and cook until crisp-tender, about 15 minutes; do not overcook. Drain well in colander and keep warm. Meanwhile, shell and finely chop eggs. Peel and crush garlic. Heat oil in small skillet, add garlic, parsley, and pine nuts and sauté until nuts are light golden, stirring frequently. Pour over cauliflower, top with chopped egg, and serve.

Cauliflower with Cheese Sauce

Photo, center

4 servings
1 cauliflower (about 1¹/₂ pounds/750 g)
Salt
For the cheese sauce
3 tablespoons (50 g) butter
¹/₄ cup (30 g) flour
1 cup (240 mL) heavy cream
¹/₂ cup (125 mL) milk
1 cup (120 g) grated Emmenthal cheese
¹/₄ teaspoon salt
Freshly ground pepper
Freshly grated nutmeg
¹/₂ cup (50 g) sliced almonds

Trim and wash cauliflower; divide into florets. Drop into large pot of boiling salted water and cook 15 to 20 minutes. Melt butter in saucepan, add flour, and stir several minutes over low heat. Whisk in cream and milk and cook until slightly thickened, 3 to 4 minutes. Season with salt, pepper, and nutmeg and simmer 2 to 3 minutes. Divide cauliflower among heatproof plates. Pour sauce over and place under broiler until top is light golden. Toast almonds in ungreased skillet until golden. Sprinkle over cauliflower and serve.

Cauliflower Gratin

Photo, top

4 servings
1 head cauliflower (about 1¹/₂ pounds/750 g)
Salt
For the sauce
5 tablespoons (90 g) butter
3 tablespoons (20 g) flour
¹/₂ cup (125 mL) heavy cream
1 cup (240 mL) meat stock
¹/₂ teaspoon salt
Freshly ground pepper
2 eggs
¹/₂ cup (60 g) freshly grated Parmesan cheese
2 tablespoons breadcrumbs

Wash and trim cauliflower; divide into florets. Drop into large pot of boiling salted water and cook 5 minutes. Drain well and keep warm. Melt 3 tablespoons (50 g) butter, add flour, and stir for several minutes over low heat. Blend in cream and meat stock, season with salt, and simmer 4 to 5 minutes, stirring. Remove from heat and whisk in eggs and cheese. Mix cauliflower into sauce. Butter oven dish and add cauliflower mixture. Melt remaining butter and mix with breadcrumbs; sprinkle over cauliflower. Bake in preheated 425°F (220°C) oven until crumbs are golden, 25 to 30 minutes. Serve hot.

Brussels Sprouts

Brussels sprouts are a relatively recent addition to the vegetable repertoire, having been first grown near Brussels about 100 years ago. In Austria they are known as *Sprossenkohl*, or sprout cabbage, because of the way the miniature heads sprout from a tall central stalk.

Be sure to buy Brussels sprouts that are bright green, firm, and tightly closed. The season for fresh Brussels sprouts is October to April, and this is the time they are at their best. The preparation is simple: Trim the base and remove any limp or discolored outer leaves. Out of season, frozen Brussels sprouts make a good substitute.

Brussels Sprouts with Cheese

Photo, bottom

4 servings
2 1/4 pounds (1 kg) Brussels sprouts
1 small onion
1/2 clove garlic
2 tablespoons vegetable oil
1 cup (240 mL) meat stock
1/2 teaspoon salt
Freshly ground pepper
Freshly grated nutmeg
2 small tomatoes
5 ounces (150 g) Gouda cheese
1/4 cup (60 mL) heavy cream
2 tablespoons chopped mixed fresh herbs (chives, parsley, basil)

Wash and trim Brussels sprouts. Peel and chop onion; peel and crush garlic. Heat oil in large saucepan. Add onion and garlic and sauté until tender. Add sprouts and meat stock; season with salt, pepper, and nutmeg. Cover and simmer 15 to 20 minutes. Blanch tomatoes briefly in boiling water; peel and cut into eighths. Stir into Brussels sprouts. Finely dice cheese and mix with cream. Pour over vegetables and sprinkle with herbs. Cover and simmer gently 5 to 10 minutes. Serve immediately.

Brussels Sprouts with Chestnuts

Photo, top

4 servings
1 1/2 pounds (700 g) Brussels sprouts
12 ounces (400 g) fresh chestnuts
3 tablespoons vegetable oil
1/2 cup (125 mL) meat stock
1/2 cup (125 mL) dry white wine
1/2 teaspoon salt
Freshly ground pepper
1 sprig each thyme, parsley and rosemary

Wash and trim Brussels sprouts. Slash chestnut shells with sharp knife. Spread chestnuts on baking sheet and bake in preheated 400°F (200°C) oven until shells burst open, 5 to 10 minutes. Peel and quarter chestnuts. Heat oil in large saucepan, add chestnuts, and sauté 2 to 3 minutes. Pour in meat stock and wine and simmer 10 minutes over medium heat. Add Brussels sprouts. Season with salt, pepper, and herbs; cover and simmer until tender but not mushy, 10 to 15 minutes; remove herb sprigs halfway through cooking and add more stock and wine if necessary.

Kale

Until fairly recent times kale was practically unknown outside northern Germany. Happily, as it becomes more familiar to Americans its popularity is spreading.

Braised Kale

Photo, top

Perfect with spicy sausages such as kielbasa or mettwurst.

4 servings
4 1/2 pounds (2 kg) kale
2 quarts (2 L) water
2 1/2 teaspoons salt
1 onion
1/4 cup (60 g) lard
2 cups (450 mL) hot meat stock
Freshly ground pepper

Wash kale well; discard stems. Cook leaves until wilted as in following recipe. Drain well and chop or grind coarsely. Peel and finely chop onion. Melt lard in large saucepan, add onion, and sauté until translucent. Add kale, stock, 1/2 teaspoon salt, and pepper. Stir through briefly, cover, and simmer 1 hour.

Variation
Grünkohl mit Pinkel

Prepare Braised Kale as in master recipe, adding several bacon slices. In Saxony and Schleswig-Holstein this is traditionally served with a brain sausage called *Brägenwurst*.

Kale One-pot

Photo, bottom

4 servings
4 1/2 pounds (2 kg) kale
2 quarts (2 L) water
Salt
1 onion
1/4 cup (60 g) lard
2 cups (450 mL) hot meat stock
Freshly ground pepper
12 ounces (400 g) beef stew meat
12 ounces (400 g) pork stew meat
2 teaspoons sweet paprika
2 tablespoons vegetable oil
2 medium carrots

Wash kale well; discard stems. Bring water to boil with 2 teaspoons salt in large pot. Add kale and cook until completely wilted, about 10 minutes. Remove and drain well; chop coarsely. Peel and finely dice onion. Melt lard in large saucepan, add onion, and sauté until translucent. Add kale, stock, 1/2 teaspoon salt, and pepper. Stir through and simmer 30 minutes. Meanwhile, cut meat into cubes and season with paprika and 1/4 teaspoon salt. Heat oil in large skillet and brown meat on all sides, then add a little hot water, cover, and braise until nearly tender, adding more water as necessary. Trim and dice carrots. When kale has cooked for 30 minutes, add meat and carrot, and braise together 30 minutes longer. Season to taste and serve.

Red Cabbage

Since there are both early and late varieties of red cabbage, it is available nearly year round (though it can be scarce from April to June). The color varies from dark red to violet.

Red Cabbage Gratin

Photo, bottom

4 servings
1 medium head red cabbage (about 2¹/₄ pounds/1 kg after trimming)
Salt
¹/₄ cup (60 mL) wine vinegar
1 medium onion
1 chili pepper
1 tart apple
7 tablespoons (100 g) butter
10 ounces (300 g) cooked smoked pork
Freshly ground pepper
13 ounces (400 g) potatoes
¹/₂ cup (125 mL) white wine
¹/₂ cup (125 mL) meat stock
¹/₂ teaspoon coarsely ground pepper
¹/₄ cup (60 g) butter, cut into small pieces

Discard wilted outer leaves from cabbage. Halve cabbage head, cut away core, and pull apart into individual leaves. Trim coarse ribs from leaves. Bring large pot of salted water to boil and add vinegar. Drop in cabbage leaves and boil 5 minutes. Drain, plunge into cold water, and drain well. Cut leaves into narrow strips. Peel and chop onion; mince chili pepper. Core and dice apple (do not peel). Melt 3¹/₂ tablespoons (50 g) butter in large saucepan, add onion, and sauté until tender. Add chopped chili and apple and cook 5 minutes. Cut pork into small cubes, add to saucepan with cabbage, and cook 10 minutes. Taste and adjust seasoning with salt and pepper. Grease baking dish with 3¹/₂ tablespoons (50 g) butter and add cabbage mixture. Peel potatoes and slice very thinly; arrange in fish-scale pattern atop cabbage. Bake in preheated 400°F (200°C) oven for 15 minutes. Pour wine and meat stock over, sprinkle with coarsely ground pepper, and dot with butter. Return to oven and bake 35 to 40 minutes longer.

Red Cabbage with Chestnuts

Photo, top

4 servings
2¹/₄ pounds (1 kg) red cabbage, trimmed
Salt
Juice of 1 lemon
1 small onion
3 tablespoons vegetable oil
1 teaspoon brown sugar
Freshly ground pepper
1 cup (240 mL) dry white wine
7 ounces (200 g) peeled chestnuts, coarsely chopped
2 Rome Beauty or other cooking apples
Meat stock (optional)

Prepare red cabbage as in previous recipe: Blanch leaves in large pot of boiling salted water with lemon juice for 3 minutes and drain well. Peel and chop onion. Heat oil in large saucepan, add onion, and sauté until tender. Stir in sugar, pepper, wine, and coarsely chopped chestnuts and cook 2 to 3 minutes over medium heat. Core and dice apples (do not peel), add to saucepan, and cook 2 to 3 minutes. Cut red cabbage leaves into strips, add to saucepan, and cook 1 hour, stirring occasionally and adding stock or water if mixture is too dry.

Green Cabbage

Cabbage is sometimes thought of as "poor people's food," though it was already a favorite on the tables of the ancient Romans. Though not trendy, perhaps, cabbage is a beloved and thrifty vegetable that is available all year round.

One classic German treatment for tender young cabbage is Bavarian. The finely chopped cabbage is braised with lots of diced bacon and a splash of meat stock, and seasoned with plenty of caraway seed.

Stuffed Whole Cabbage

4 servings
1 head of cabbage (about 2 1/2 pounds/1200 g)
Salt
1 small onion
2 tablespoons vegetable oil
2 tablespoons chopped fresh parsley
12 ounces (400 g) mixed ground meat
1 egg
1 tablespoon capers
Freshly ground pepper
2 quarts (2 L) beef or veal stock

Trim cabbage and blanch whole head in large pot of boiling salted water until ribs of outer leaves are flexible, about 10 to 15 minutes. Lift cabbage out of water and drain well.

Photo 1: Lay cabbage on cotton netting or cheesecloth and carefully bend outer leaves away from head without breaking. Cut out inner leaves and chop finely.

Photo 2: Peel and finely dice onion. Heat oil in skillet, add onion and parsley, and sauté until onion is transparent; cool. Combine meat, egg, onion mixture, capers, and chopped cabbage in large bowl and mix well, seasoning with salt and pepper.

Photo 3: Place cabbage, in netting, in bowl large enough to hold it comfortably. Spoon meat stuffing into center, mounding top to the original size and shape of the cabbage.

Photo 4: Fold outer leaves over stuffing and carefully press down; the stuffing must be completely covered, and the cabbage should look as it did before center was removed.

Photo 5: Fasten netting at top of cabbage by tying with string. Bring meat stock to boil in pot large enough to hold cabbage. Lower cabbage into pot with netting. Cover partially and simmer gently over low heat 2 to 3 hours.

Insert large fork into netting and lift cabbage out of pot; transfer to large serving bowl. Cut netting open at top and drape over sides of bowl. Invert onto large plate and remove netting (cabbage will be upside down), then reinvert cabbage back into bowl.

Photo 6: Cut cabbage into quarters directly in bowl. Accompany each serving with a spoonful or two of the broth.

Sauerkraut

In southern Germany and Alsace, sauerkraut can virtually be considered the national dish.

Hungarian Sauerkraut

Serve with boiled potatoes sprinkled with caraway seed.

4 to 6 servings
2 slices (50 g) bacon
1 1/2 pounds (750 g) sauerkraut
1 cup (240 mL) white wine
1 bay leaf
1/2 teaspoon salt
Freshly ground pepper
For the filling
1 small onion
2 tablespoons (30 g) lard
10 ounces (300 g) ground pork
2 tablespoons tomato paste
2 teaspoons sweet paprika
1/2 teaspoon salt
5 ounces (150 g) smoked sausage
3/4 cup (200 g) sour cream
8 strips (150 g) bacon

Finely dice bacon and sauté in large saucepan until fat is rendered. Add sauerkraut, wine, bay leaf, salt, and pepper and simmer until liquid is completely evaporated, about 20 minutes.

For the filling, peel and chop onion. Melt lard in skillet, add onion, and sauté until lightly browned. Stir in ground meat, tomato paste, paprika, and salt and cook briefly over medium-high heat. Thinly slice sausage and add to skillet.

Spread half of sauerkraut in baking dish and top evenly with filling. Cover with remaining sauerkraut and pour sour cream over. Arrange bacon slices on top. Bake in preheated 400°F (200°C) oven 30 to 40 minutes.

Alsatian Wine Kraut

Not illustrated

A delicious and versatile side dish.

4 servings
3 pounds (1500 g) sauerkraut
1 onion
2 whole cloves
1 clove garlic
5 juniper berries
1 cup (240 mL) dry Alsatian white wine
6 tablespoons (100 g) lard or goose fat
Salt (optional)
Water or meat stock (optional)

Rinse sauerkraut well in cold water and drain well. Squeeze out as much water as possible. Transfer to large nonaluminum saucepan, fluffing strands with hands. Peel onion and stud with the cloves; add to sauerkraut with peeled whole garlic clove and juniper berries. Pour white wine over and add fat. Season lightly with salt if sauerkraut is very mild. Cover and simmer 1 hour over medium heat, stirring occasionally and adding water or meat stock if mixture dries out. Reduce heat to very low and continue cooking at a slow simmer for 1 1/2 to 2 hours longer.

Kohlrabi

Kohlrabi is available nearly year round. The greenhouse-grown type starts appearing in February; outdoor-harvested kohlrabi starts in May or June and continues until late fall.

Kohlrabi One-pot

Photo, bottom

4 servings
3 pounds (1500 g) kohlrabi with tops
1 generous pound (500 g) boiling potatoes
3 medium carrots
1 small onion
1/2 clove garlic
1/4 cup (60 mL) vegetable oil
1 cup (240 mL) chicken stock
2 tablespoons chopped mixed fresh herbs (parsley, chives, basil and, optionally, fennel tops)
Freshly ground pepper
1/2 to 1 teaspoon salt

Remove tops from kohlrabi, reserving small, tender leaves. Peel bulbs and cut into sticks 3/8 inch (1 cm) thick. Peel and coarsely dice potatoes. Scrub carrots under running water, then cut into sticks the size of kohlrabi. Peel and chop onion; peel and crush garlic. Heat oil in large saucepan, add onion and garlic, and sauté until tender. Add potato cubes, pour chicken stock over, and simmer 5 minutes over medium heat. Add kohlrabi and carrot sticks, pouring in a bit more chicken stock if mixture seems dry. Simmer until vegetables are tender but not mushy, 15 to 20 minutes, testing frequently toward end of cooking time. Finely chop herbs and reserved kohlrabi leaves and add to vegetables shortly before end of cooking, at the same time seasoning with salt and pepper.

Kohlrabi Skillet Supper

Photo, top

4 servings
3 pounds (1500 g) kohlrabi with tops
1 small onion
1 clove garlic
1 small carrot
1 small parsley root
3 tablespoons (40 g) butter
12 ounces (400 g) mixed ground meat
1/2 teaspoon salt
Freshly ground pepper
1 small bell pepper, diced
1 egg yolk
1 cup (50 g) breadcrumbs
1 tablespoon chopped fresh parsley
1/2 cup (125 mL) heavy cream

Peel kohlrabi and cut into sticks 3/8 inch (1 cm) thick. Peel and chop onion; peel and crush garlic. Trim and dice carrot and parsley root. Melt butter in small skillet. Add onion, garlic, carrot, and parsley root and sauté until tender. Combine meat, salt, pepper, diced bell pepper, and onion mixture in bowl. Add egg yolk and mix well.

Grease baking dish well, then sprinkle with breadcrumbs. Spread half of kohlrabi in dish. Top with meat mixture, smoothing top, then cover with remaining kohlrabi. Sprinkle with parsley and pour cream over. Bake in preheated 400°F (200°C) oven 40 to 50 minutes, brushing top with a bit of melted butter if it browns too quickly.

Chinese Cabbage

First cultivated in the West around the turn of the century, Chinese cabbage gained real popularity only after the second World War. Though it is outstanding as a salad green, the Chinese use it exclusively as a vegetable. Its main season is from August through February. Chinese cabbage may be sold as either bok choy or napa (celery) cabbage. Pictured here is napa (celery) cabbage.

Chinese Cabbage Rolls

Photo, bottom

4 servings
1 cup (240 mL) milk
3½ tablespoons (40 g) rice
2 small onions
4 ounces (150 g) boneless beef
6 ounces (150 g) boneless pork
6 ounces (150 g) boneless lamb
1 ounce (30 g) pancetta or bacon (if using bacon, blanch briefly to reduce smoky taste)
1 clove garlic
3 tablespoons chopped fresh parsley
Pinch each of dried oregano and dried basil
1 egg
Salt and freshly ground pepper
12 large celery cabbage leaves
1 cup (240 mL) beef stock

Scald milk, stir in rice, and simmer over very low heat until rice is tender, about 30 minutes. Peel and quarter onions. Grind meats, pancetta, and onion quarters in meat grinder. Peel and crush garlic. Combine meat mixture, garlic, herbs, egg, rice, salt, and pepper and mix well. Blanch cabbage leaves briefly in boiling water, drain, and plunge into cold water to stop cooking process; drain well. Spread out leaves on work surface and cut out thick end of central rib using wedge-shaped cut. Divide meat mixture into 12 equal-size balls or ovals and place each near base of 1 cabbage leaf. Roll up leaf 2/3 of the way, then tuck in sides and continue rolling to completely enclose filling. Butter ovenproof skillet or baking dish. Arrange cabbage rolls in skillet and pour beef stock over. Bake in preheated 350°F (175°C) oven until lightly browned, about 40 minutes.

Chinese Cabbage with Bacon

Photo, top

4 servings
2¼ pounds (1 kg) Chinese cabbage
1 onion
3 tablespoons (40 g) lard
10 ounces (300 g) thickly sliced bacon
2 cups (450 mL) meat stock
2 medium carrots
3 medium leeks
1 generous pound (500 g) boiling potatoes
Salt and freshly ground pepper
Pinch of sweet paprika

Trim cabbage and cut into coarse strips; wash and drain well. Peel and chop onion. Cut each bacon strip into several pieces. Melt lard in saucepan, add bacon, and sauté until lightly browned. Add onion and sauté until translucent. Pour in meat stock, cover, and simmer 30 minutes. Trim and slice carrots and leeks; peel and dice potatoes. Add cabbage, carrot, leek, and potato to saucepan and simmer 30 minutes longer. Just before serving, season with salt, pepper, and paprika.

EXOTIC VEGETABLES

Indian Vegetables

The most characteristic feature of Indian cooking is its extraordinary use of spices. Indian cooks are particularly adept with vegetables; many Indians are vegetarian, and their vegetable curries are flavorful enough to convert the most determined meat eater. A true Indian spice mixture has little to do with the curry powder sold in Western markets; though convenient, this canned substitute cannot replace a blend of individual spices.

Vegetable Curry

A sprinkling of freshly grated coconut rounds out this dish beautifully. Packaged coconut is too chewy and not nearly flavorful enough. In a pinch, you can use packaged coconut that has been soaked for several hours in warm water, but it will not compare with fresh.

4 servings
1 1/2 pounds (750 g) boiling potatoes
Salt
1 small onion
2 cloves garlic
2 medium tomatoes
1 large cucumber
2 stalks celery
3 tablespoons vegetable oil
1 teaspoon caraway seed
1 teaspoon cumin seed
1/2 teaspoon turmeric
1/2 teaspoon ground coriander
1/4 teaspoon freshly ground pepper
2 chili peppers
2 knobs ginger root
1/2 cup (125 mL) meat stock
7 ounces (200 g) okra
5 ounces (150 g) fresh or frozen peas
Optional
1 tablespoon chopped cilantro or parsley
1/2 cup grated fresh coconut

Peel and dice potatoes; simmer in salted water until half cooked. Drain well. Peel and chop onion; peel and crush garlic. Blanch tomatoes briefly in boiling water. Peel, halve, and seed tomatoes; cut into pieces. Peel cucumber and halve lengthwise; scoop out seeds and dice flesh. Cut celery into very thin strips. Heat oil in large saucepan. Add caraway and cumin seed and roast 2 to 3 minutes, stirring constantly and being careful not to let spices burn. Add onion and garlic and sauté 2 minutes. Add celery strips and cook for 2 minutes, then stir in turmeric, coriander, and pepper.

Halve chili peppers, carefully remove seeds, and chop peppers finely. Peel and finely dice ginger. Add peppers and ginger to saucepan with tomato, cucumber, and meat stock and simmer 5 minutes. Meanwhile, wash okra and trim stem ends; halve pods lengthwise or cut into pieces. Add to saucepan and simmer 5 minutes. Add peas and potato cubes and cook just until potatoes are tender. Sprinkle with chopped cilantro or parsley and coconut and serve immediately.

Chinese Vegetables

No cuisine in the world is prepared with more attention to appearance and detail than Chinese. This is especially true of vegetables, which are cut into small pieces and stir-fried very quickly over the highest possible heat. The preferred cooking pan is a round, thin-sided iron wok, which conducts heat quickly; a flat-bottomed skillet is a poor substitute. Chinese markets also sell a wide spatula-like implement for tossing the ingredients during stir-frying; it is slightly rounded to conform well to the shape of the wok.

The wok's spherical form makes very little cooking oil necessary. Many Chinese recipes also require little in the way of seasoning, because with quick, careful cooking the flavor of the vegetables themselves stays at its best.

Mixed Vegetable Stir-fry

Serve with rice or noodles, which should be cooked and ready the moment the vegetables come off the heat. You may also add chicken, beef, or pork to the vegetable mixture. Slice it into fine strips and stir-fry in the wok over very high heat with a little oil and a sprinkling of salt. Remove from the wok and keep warm, then cook the vegetables according to the recipe and mix in the cooked poultry or meat shortly before serving.

4 servings
12 Chinese dried mushrooms
2 cups (450 mL) hot water
4 green onions
2 large celery stalks, leaves trimmed
3 medium carrots
1 large zucchini
1 red bell pepper
1 can (10 ounces/300 g) bamboo shoots
1 clove garlic
2 knobs ginger root
1/4 cup (60 mL) peanut oil
1/2 teaspoon salt
1 teaspoon sugar
3 tablespoons dark soy sauce
Freshly ground pepper
3 ounces (100 g) bean sprouts

Soak dried mushrooms in the hot water for about 30 minutes. Cut away stems and squeeze excess water from caps. Reserve soaking liquid. Trim away green onion tops. Cut onions into pieces about 1 1/4 inches (3 cm) long; cut pieces into thin strips. Trim bottom end of each celery stalk; cut celery into 1 1/4- to 1 1/2-inch (3- to 4-cm) pieces, then into strips. Peel carrots and cut into thin sticks. Scrub and trim zucchini, slice thinly and halve slices if large. Halve, stem, and seed bell pepper; cut into strips. Drain bamboo shoots and cut into sticks. Peel, and crush garlic; peel and mince ginger. (Be sure to prepare all vegetables beforehand, as the cooking cannot be interrupted once it is started.)

Heat oil in wok over highest possible heat. Add garlic and ginger and stir-fry briefly. Add onion and celery strips and stir-fry 2 minutes. Add mushrooms, carrots, zucchini, and pepper strips and stir-fry 3 to 4 minutes. Pour in 1/2 cup (125 mL) mushroom soaking liquid and boil 5 to 6 minutes. Season with salt, sugar, soy sauce, and pepper. Add bamboo shoots and bean sprouts and stir-fry 2 to 3 minutes longer. Serve immediately.

METRIC—IMPERIAL CONVERSION TABLE

Note that the recipes in this book feature both U.S. customary and metric measurements. For cooks in Great Britain, Canada, and Australia, note the following information for imperial measurements. If you are familiar with metric measurements, then we recommend you follow those, incorporated into every recipe. If not, then use these conversions to achieve best results. Bear in mind that ingredients such as flour vary greatly and you will have to make some adjustments.

Liquid Measures

The British cup is larger than the American. The Australian cup is smaller than the British but a little larger than the American. Use the following cup measurements for liquids, making the adjustments as indicated.

U.S.	1 cup (236 ml)
British and Canadian	1 cup (284 ml)—adjust measurement to $1/4$ pint + 2 tablespoons
Australian	1 cup (250 ml)—adjust measurement to $1/4$ pint

Weight and Volume Measures

U.S. cooking procedures usually measure certain items by volume, although in other countries these items are often measured by weight. Here are some approximate equivalents for basic items.

	U.S. Customary	Metric	Imperial
Butter	1 cup	250 g	8 ounces
	$1/2$ cup	125 g	4 ounces
	$1/4$ cup	62 g	2 ounces
	1 tablespoon	15 g	$1/2$ ounce
Flour (sifted all-purpose or plain)	1 cup	128 g	$4^{1}/_4$ ounces
	$1/2$ cup	60 g	$2^{1}/_8$ ounces
	$1/4$ cup	32 g	1 ounce
Sugar (caster)	1 cup	240 g	8 ounces
	$1/2$ cup	120 g	4 ounces
	1 tablespoon	15 g	$1/2$ ounce
Chopped vegetables	1 cup	115 g	4 ounces
	$1/2$ cup	60 g	2 ounces
Chopped meats or fish	1 cup	225 g	8 ounces
	$1/2$ cup	110 g	4 ounces

INDEX

Christian Teubner is a highly sought-after photographer specializing in food photography. His work conveys the special magic and fun of cooking, whether he is picturing soups, main courses, or desserts. He again shows his love of cooking in this beautifully illustrated collection of his favorite recipes.